W9-BAB-949

EATING MUD CRABS IN KANDAHAR

CALIFORNIA STUDIES IN FOOD AND CULTURE

DARRA GOLDSTEIN, EDITOR

EATING MUD CRABS
~IN KANDAHAR~

STORIES OF FOOD DURING WARTIME
BY THE WORLD'S LEADING CORRESPONDENTS

EDITED BY **MATT McALLESTER**

UNIVERSITY OF CALIFORNIA PRESS BERKELEY LOS ANGELES LONDON

University of California Press, one of the most distinguished university presses in the United States, enriches lives around the world by advancing scholarship in the humanities, social sciences, and natural sciences. Its activities are supported by the UC Press Foundation and by philanthropic contributions from individuals and institutions. For more information, visit www.ucpress.edu.

University of California Press
Berkeley and Los Angeles, California

University of California Press, Ltd.
London, England

Library of Congress Cataloging-in-Publication Data
Eating mud crabs in Kandahar : stories of food during wartime by the world's leading correspondents / edited by Matt McAllester.
     p. cm.—(California studies in food and culture; 31)
  ISBN 978-0-520-26867-8 (cloth : alk. paper)
    1. Survival and emergency rations—Anecdotes. 2. Food habits—Anecdotes.
3. War correspondents—Anecdotes. 4. Foreign journalists—Anecdotes. 5. War—
Social aspects—Anecdotes. I. McAllester, Matthew, 1969–
  TX357.E286 2011
  394.1'2—dc23

2011017737

Manufactured in the United States of America

20 19 18 17 16 15 14 13 12 11
10 9 8 7 6 5 4 3 2 1

In keeping with a commitment to support environmentally responsible and sustainable printing practices, UC Press has printed this book on Natures Book, a fiber that contains 30% post-consumer waste and meets the minimum requirements of ANSI/NISO Z39.48–1992 (R 1997) (*Permanence of Paper*).

FOR HARRY

AND

FOR TIM HETHERINGTON, 1970–2011

CONTENTS

THE NAME OF THE
THIRD CHICKEN
~KOSOVO~

MATT McALLESTER

"WHAT DO YOU HAVE TO EAT?" I ASKED THE KOSOVAR ALBANIAN woman, at whose wooden hut in the snow-covered Mountains of the Damned I had just arrived, in the company of her son, another reporter, two photographers, and a translator.

Actually, I didn't ask her directly. I asked the other reporter, Philip Sherwell, who spoke German. He then asked the question of the elderly lady's son, Haki, because he too spoke German. He then asked the lady, whose name was Zejnepe, in Albanian. And back, through Haki and Philip and two languages I did not understand, came the answer.

"We have some flour and oil for making bread," Zejnepe said.

"What else do you have?" I asked, looking around at a few other jars and tins on a shelf that lined the walls of the shepherd's hut, which was heated with a wood-burning stove. We were warming our frozen bare feet and sodden socks and boots in front of the stove. It was late April 1999 and we had just hiked from the small Yugoslav republic of Montenegro through Serb-controlled territory, at some risk, to visit this old lady who had sworn she would rather be killed than leave Kosovo. Living with her in the tiny hut were five other adult relatives, three elderly, two young. The six of us who had just arrived were exhausted—except for Haki, who strolled through the snow and over the mountains as if he was going down to get coffee from the corner store. Philip and I had not known each other long. We worked for different newspapers and were not used to working together. Our exhaustion, coupled with my need to rely on him as a translator, was creating a timbre of irritation in the hut as we continued this crucial interview, which we knew would constitute one of the only firsthand accounts of life inside Serb-controlled Kosovo.

Philip asked Haki, who asked Zejnepe what else they had. Zejnepe told Haki, who told Philip, who told me the answer.

"Coffee and sugar," Philip said, and I wrote that down in my notebook.

"Can we move on?" he added. He had stopped writing in his notebook.

"In a minute," I said. "Could you ask her if they have any other source of food? They can't just be surviving on bread and coffee."

Philip paused, took a deep breath, and asked Haki, who asked Zejnepe my question.

"Every day her nephew, Jeton, goes down the hill to where they keep a cow tethered, and he milks it and brings back the milk," Philip said, and I stared at my notebook and wrote down what he had said and tried not to look at him.

"Matt, do you mind if we actually move on to the reason we're here and ask about Serbian ethnic cleansing rather than performing an audit of her larder?" Philip asked.

"Didn't I see some chickens outside?" I asked.

"Yes, you did," Philip said, without bothering to ask Haki, given that we had unquestionably seen chickens outside the hut pecking in the muddy snow.

"Could you ask her how many chickens she has?" I said.

Philip put down his notebook.

"And would you like me to ask her the name of the third chicken?"

"No, never mind," I said, realizing that my volunteer translator had just resigned.

"Thank you," Philip said, asking a question of his own.

In the years since, Philip and I have often laughed about the name of the third chicken, but I can also still see why the precise number of Zejnepe's fowl seemed important to me then. Zejnepe and her relatives looked hungry and drawn. The chickens bought these people time. In the grassy plain that spread out below the snowy mountains—gazing down from the mountains at the plain was like looking at spring from midwinter—the Serbian paramilitary groups usually showed little mercy to remaining Albanians. There was no extra food to be had up here in the mountains. In fact, Jeton and his equally brave father, Emrush, made occasional nighttime excursions down to the plain to get more flour from their abandoned house, which was in a village within view. They had checked the refrigerator, and everything inside had gone off. Philip, his photographer colleague, Julian Simmonds, and I debated going with Jeton on his next journey to get flour, but we decided it was too dangerous. It would have been a nighttime raid to get an ingredient.

War had very rapidly taken a lot from these people: their homes, their freedom of movement, and Zejnepe's husband, who had been shot dead by Serbs. And what they were left with was basic shelter, a source of heat, each other, and some larder supplies. Flour, oil, milk, coffee, sugar, eggs, perhaps some chicken meat. Food meant survival, which meant the Serbs had not yet won.

Not all wars are fought over food supplies or other natural resources—although many are—but in all wars food plays a significant role. At some stage in a day's fighting, a soldier has to roll behind the wall he is using for shelter to open his army-issue rations. In a day of explaining to her children why they can't go home yet, a refugee mother has to feed them two or three times. In a day of reporting on a conflict, no matter where in the world, a correspondent has to fuel up as well. No matter what role you have in a conflict, you have to step out of it for at least a few minutes every day to have breakfast, lunch, dinner—or a piece of bread. Meals put war on hold, even if the guns are still firing outside. And in these moments families re-group, friends tell stories of the day so far and exchange crucial informa-tion, and new friends are made; sharing a meal with a stranger is the best way to make you strangers no longer. Amid the awfulness of war, food is a rare, regular source of comfort. And when there is comfort, there is open-ness. Confidences are shared and jokes cracked. Philip is one of my dearest friends, and many of our bonding moments came over not-very-good meals in places where there was fighting, beginning there in the mountains as we shared bread—with shame but great gratitude—that Zejnepe and her fam-ily gave us.

Many foreign correspondents are somewhat food-obsessed. Food can be a rare source of comfort on the road. But even those who don't carry pepper mills in their backpacks, as my friend Ed Gargan does, are inevitably aware of how food can be a matter of life or death and how meals can reveal se-crets. The writers in this collection have reached into their memories and notebooks to unearth stories about food they have never had a chance to write before, or were never able to expand upon in the newspapers or maga-zines that employ them. Not all of the stories take place, strictly speaking, in war zones, but the shadow of conflict or the threat of violence or oppres-sion looms in all.

The writers are all British or American print journalists who are among the world's greatest chroniclers of recent conflicts. The stories they tell mostly take place between that momentous year of change, 1989, and 2009—for little reason other than organizational neatness. They offer stories of the appetites of the powerful—Benazir Bhutto, Ariel Sharon, Kim Jong Il—and of the powerless and, in some cases, starving. There are personal stories, about the birth and illness of a beloved son and about understanding the country of Georgia through one great friend, and there are more traditional reported stories, about the transformative power of food in China and the obsession among the starving millions of North Korea with locating sources of nutrition. And alongside the stories of food, there is a story of drink—

4

bar owner Scott Anderson's tale of drinking his way into the heart of the Irish Republican Army's fund-raising crew.

I have sought out stories from all of the troubled corners of the world, but perhaps inevitably three writers tell stories of Afghanistan and three of Israel and the Palestinian Territories: important conflicts that carry on to this day.

Amid the tragedy and the violence there are jokes, and great goodwill. And, perhaps, a little more humanity than we can usually slip into our newspaper and magazine stories.

Zejnepe never left Kosovo. Sometime between our visit and the end of the war, Serbian soldiers or paramilitary troops shot her dead along with two of the other elderly people in the hut. Jeton, Haki, and his brother Naim found her body on the mountainside as the snow melted. After the war I visited her grave with them on a gentle sunny morning. After we stood in silence for a while, they took me home to their village. They had prepared lunch.

~PART ONE~
SURVIVAL RATIONS

NIGHT LIGHT

~EL SALVADOR AND HAITI~

LEE HOCKSTADER

I AM SITTING IN MY APARTMENT AT NIGHT, ALONE AND IN THE DARK. In San Salvador, electricity is as fickle as the weather—you take what you get. Tonight there is none, so I sit in the dark.

In the dark but not in silence. Directly above my roof, maybe a hundred yards overhead, a Salvadoran army helicopter gunship hovers, its blades thudding against the thick tropical heat. The helicopter's gunner is firing staccato cannon bursts into the hills a mile away, where the guerrillas make camp just outside the capital. Each burst belches out an angry, mechanical growl, very loud: *Bbrrrr!* Between cannon bursts I hear a little girl crying, having been jolted from her sleep in the apartment across the hall. Her parents, Seventh Day Adventist missionaries who feed me home-cooked meals and proselytize me at the dessert course, are trying to comfort her. Their voices are murmurs through the walls.

I have a battery-operated lantern that emits just enough mottled, bluish light for me to avoid bumping into walls as I navigate my little apartment. I set it on the kitchen counter so it illuminates the gas stove and fry some ham and eggs. I'm hungry, and the cooking gives me something to do besides sit and listen to the cannon fire overhead.

Bbbrrrr!

I eat my eggs, sopping up yolk with stale bread. I try to read the paper but the light's no good; I can't make out the print.

My apartment, on the ground floor, is cheerless and shabby, furnished with rattan chairs and table. In the living room, louvered glass slats give out on an overgrown garden that frames a miniature, scum-crusted pool. Vermin of every description enter my apartment through the glass slats, which don't close convincingly. The living room's damp shag carpet is alive with beetles and crickets and slugs. Except in bed, I keep my shoes on at all times. If I were in El Salvador more often than a few days every month or two, between reporting trips to Haiti, Nicaragua, Cuba, Guatemala, or Honduras, I'd probably move to a better place.

Bbbrrrr!

The helicopter is still going at it. Sleep is impossible, and it's not late anyway. If I had friends in El Salvador I could go out, but after just a few months here the people I do know—colleagues whose offices flank mine in an office building downtown—aren't really friends. Besides, I have no car here, and taxis are scarce when the gunship is doing its work.

Sending me off on my three-year assignment, my editor in Washington had told me I should think of myself as a sort of one-man news-gathering hub for Central America and the Caribbean—the eyes and ears of a great metropolitan newspaper. He said I should be better informed than the local CIA station chiefs, and have a wider range of contacts. At the moment, I might as well be locked in a sensory-deprivation tank.

I lean back from the table in my folding chair and mutter, *What the fuck!* I'm going nuts. I'm stuck. I can't read. There's no light. I carry the lantern back into the kitchen and fling open the cabinet and fridge doors. What I find is mildly encouraging, thanks to a recent foraging trip to Miami. There is a French garlic sausage. Some packets of Japanese rice crackers, spicy little crescents flecked with red pepper. A jar of Moroccan green olives. Then I remember that Doña Marta, my housekeeper, has left me a batch of her refried beans, irresistibly oily and black as tar, made fresh that morning. I find them on a plate under waxed paper. And there is beer, still cool in the lifeless fridge. This is good. This is solace. I have the makings here of a feast.

I'd begged to be a foreign correspondent, and dreamed of it, but my sketchy fantasies hadn't included gunfire and power outages and loneliness. Ambition, restlessness, a vague idea that it would be good to be far from editors and paid to travel the world—this is what had led me, like generations of correspondents before me, to apply. At my newspaper, the *Washington Post,* three postings were available—Germany, India, and Central America. When the foreign editor had asked my preference I'd more or less shrugged, saying I'd be thrilled to go anywhere.

Now, months later, I've arrived in Central America at a pivotal moment, just as communism and the Cold War are unraveling. The Soviet Union, having financed and sponsored the region's leftist combatants in order to bleed the United States, has suddenly disappeared from the world stage. Like a slow leak from a balloon, the logic is seeping out of two decades of proxy wars, death squads, massacres, and fraternal bloodbaths.

But it's harder to stop the armed young men who know nothing but fighting and killing. The momentum of revenge impels them; repurposing them will take time.

As I work my beat, traveling among Salvador, Nicaragua, Honduras, Guatemala, and Haiti, I'm struck by the relentless grimness that has settled in after so many seasons of violence and despair. In Nicaragua, where the United States has spent billions arming and equipping the Contra rebels, families are bitterly divided and the economy lies in ruins; there are just two or three working elevators in the entire country. Honduras, equally bleak, is crawling with CIA agents who are busy tracking and manipulating the region's various small wars. In Guatemala, a team of American forensic specialists is digging up the remains of leftists murdered by death squads. Moving among these countries is grinding and joyless.

Everything besides work feels like a welcome escape, and nothing more so than food. In Nicaragua, my colleagues and I eat in open-air restaurants after the day's heat has eased. We trade rumors and feast on skirt steaks with *chimichurri* sauce served with huge platters of French fries. We eat bull's testicles *a la parilla,* sizzling from the grill, and garlicky shrimp and baby eels drowning in olive oil.

The bills are a pittance, just ten or fifteen dollars a person. But inflation has atomized the local currency, so to pay for dinner we all produce stacks of pesos whose huge denominations obscure their actual value, which is close to zero. Just counting it all takes forever—it's like paying with pennies, only this is paper money—and by the time we've finished, the table is covered with an impressive dune of cash. The photographers climb up on chairs to take pictures of this hillock of nearly worthless bills.

In Salvador, I develop an unhealthy addiction to Pollo Campero, a chain of fried chicken joints whose secret recipe, near as I can tell, involves nothing but salt. On trips to the countryside to track down the guerrillas, I stuff my backpack with *pupusas revueltas,* pillowy corn tortillas filled with beans, cheese, and meat, the ubiquitous street food of San Salvador.

As comfort food this is all fine, but it provides meager relief. There is bloodshed and trauma everywhere, and the days are blood-spattered and draining. I've always loved to eat, but after a while, my relationship with food is transformed. It's not just that I enjoy food; I am needy. For me, food becomes like alcohol, and consuming it is a diversion that helps keep me sane. I eat partly in hope of forgetting what I've seen, and remembering what pleasure feels like.

On the morning after the meal in my darkened apartment, I am out reporting in San Salvador with a colleague when his pager buzzes: six priests have been murdered overnight at the nation's preeminent university. We race across town and arrive before the police. Four of the priests are lying facedown on their front lawn, their arms splayed at weird angles. Two of them are draped in their nightshirts; the others have on T-shirts or pajamas. They're wearing slippers. One priest is tall; his white gown is crumpled, its hem bunched at his thighs. Just beyond him lies a second priest—dark T-shirt, lighter pants. A third is to the left, and a fourth is nearly skull-to-skull with the third. Two more are inside the house.

On the lawn, the brains of two of the men have been blown cleanly from their heads by the impact of assault rifles fired at close range. Their skulls, emptied of their contents, are sallow, deflated, and misshapen. I stare, then turn away and squeeze my eyes shut tight. I am dizzy and breathless.

Just a few months earlier I'd been in Washington, D.C., living with my girlfriend, wearing bow ties to work, trying out a beard, playing hoops on weekends, cooking elaborate meals—soufflés, Chinese pot stickers, chicken Kiev. I was a dandy, self-absorbed; I'd seen nothing very terrible. Now I am here on this lawn, with these dead priests, staring, looking away, my mouth so dry I can barely swallow. *So this is what evil looks like,* I think.

The priests were Salvadoran leftists, liberation theologists, men of peace. They were the most famous intellectuals in the country—one the university's rector, another the vice-rector, another a noted sociologist whom I'd interviewed weeks before, a kind man, self-effacing, intelligent. They had been taken from the beds where they slept, dragged into the yard of their residence, and executed by Salvadoran army troops. The army brass, fierce anticommunists, have long hated the Jesuits, whom they regard as the guerrillas' intellectual godfathers.

By mid-morning, the sun is blinding. The bystanders at the Jesuits' house, standing like sentries and gawking at the bodies, cast stocky shadows. The sun has etched dark shadow-rims around the bodies, too, delineating them. It is hot, suffocating.

We get another pager message, this time about a Mexican cameraman, a colleague, who is missing. We set out in a convoy of media vehicles—Jeeps and Land Cruisers with "TV" in big letters taped to the windows like a talisman to repel bullets. There is shooting everywhere—the guerrillas have stormed the capital, capturing chic neighborhoods and slums—and the city is a mess. Shattered glass carpets the sidewalks. The streets are an obstacle course of fallen utility poles and tangled bouquets of power lines. No one knows which wires might electrocute you.

We pile out of our cars in the neighborhood where the cameraman was last seen—a rundown school with its trash-strewn playing field, some abandoned-looking small apartment buildings—and start looking around. It is spookily quiet. We see no one. Then gunfire erupts. *Fuck!* I throw myself to the pavement and roll to the curb, the only bit of cover available, and my colleagues do the same, all of us piled up, panting, cursing. We can't tell where the shooting is coming from, whether we're the target or simply caught in the crossfire, but the bullets are just over our heads, buzzing like angry hornets. My teeth, my fists, my jaw, my eyes, my ass, my whole body is clenched in terror, and I press my face into the dirt and dog shit at the curb. I have never been religious, but now I am praying: *Pleasegodpleasepleasepleasepleasegod.*

My beat for the newspaper includes both Central America and the Caribbean, but no air connections link them directly. To fly from El Salvador or Nicaragua to, say, Cuba or Haiti, you have to go through Miami. My habit is to stay a few days in transit with my notes and laundry and receipts strewn over the floor of my hotel room.

I do my expense accounts, work, order room service, see a few friends, try to decompress. But I am jumpy and short-tempered—I find myself flinching at loud noises. I take a stab at talking about the chaos I've witnessed, describing my fear, the paralyzing proximity of gunfire and bullets. It doesn't help. Over drinks with a friend at the News Café in South Beach, bathed in late-afternoon sunshine and gazing at the young models sauntering down the sidewalk, I find it impossible to recount the scene of the dead priests, or convey the ordeal that followed. It's not beyond my powers of description; it's just too starkly out of context. Except for other correspondents, no one can relate. No one wants to hear it.

I live nowhere that is really home, my friends are far away, and the places I work are joyless and terrorized. The idea that a good meal can wash away the taste of terror is ridiculous. But my thoughts keep wandering in that direction. I want a blowout meal, something spectacular. I want it as balm, as a diversion, as fortification, as an escape. I find the best Italian restaurant in town, a sedate place in Coral Gables, take a table on my own, and start ordering. I order the San Daniele prosciutto and buffalo mozzarella and tiny pungent olives. I order littleneck clams, risotto with saffron, and a Roman chicory salad. The waiter nods and starts back to the kitchen, but I smile ruefully and tell him, *Sorry, I'm not quite done.* I order more—veal with mushrooms and a good bottle of Barolo. I eat slowly, delighting in the meal. This is gluttony, pure and simple, but I'm not just hungry for the food; I'm hungry for pleasure in the vague hope that it may neutralize some of what I've seen.

The trip to Florida will be short, I know. There is news in Haiti—a power grab by the army, a bloody interlude, nocturnal gangs roaming the capital. But I crave some touchstone of normalcy and home. So in the few days I have in Florida I find it with my grandparents, well into their seventies, who live in a retirement community in Boca Raton.

The drive from Miami to Boca is under an hour, and I know exactly what to expect when I get to my grandparents' condo. My grandmother will have the front door open, and she will be standing just behind the screen, surveying the parking lot, so by the time I park and step out of my car she will be out at the second-floor railing, beaming and bellowing my name.

She is tiny and shrunken and fragile, bony in my arms. Her arthritic hands are knobby and liver-spotted.

"Did you drive on I-95?"

She is terribly anxious, and I can hear the fear in her voice.

"Of course, Nana, there's no other way to go."

"The TV said there are crazy people shooting at cars there! It happened just a few weeks ago. Honey, I wish you wouldn't go on that road, such crazy people."

My grandparents—dotty, off-kilter, fussy, familiar—are well past their prime. Listening to their patter is like revisiting the sound track of my childhood.

They live a mile from the beach but never go. They spend their days indoors, avoiding the sun, shuttling between doctors and hospitals. With visitors the talk runs to health problems, funerals, obituaries, taxes, and restaurants. My grandparents love to eat.

We set off for the early-bird special at a French place, and on our way they introduce me to neighbors who recognize me from my grandparents' bragging.

"The foreign correspondent! How are you, foreign correspondent?" The neighbors shout so loudly that I take a step back.

My grandmother grips my arm as she shuffles to the car. I insist on driving. Their own driving is insanely slow and they notice absolutely nothing on the road that's not directly in front of them, slow-moving, and very large. I make a point of sticking to the speed limit, which requires some effort. They both tell me to slow down anyway.

The restaurant is busy with early birds: retirees who favor pastel sport shirts, beltless pants they call slacks, and white patent leather shoes with rubber soles. Sun streams in the restaurant windows. It doesn't feel like dinnertime, but I have a huge appetite nonetheless. The early bird special— country pâté set on a nest of hydroponic lettuce, poached lobster dabbed with a jarring citrus glaze, gooey chocolate mousse crowned with a maraschino cherry—is Floridian French. It's a bizarre hybrid, and a weird sendoff. The next morning I get a southbound flight, and in a few hours I am away from south Florida's strip malls and sprinklers and shuffling retirees. Suddenly, I'm in another world altogether.

On my very first trip to Haiti, I take a walk along the seafront a few blocks from downtown Port-au-Prince. A traffic jam fouls the air with clouds of exhaust fumes so thick I have to breathe through my shirtsleeve. The streets teem with legless beggars and deformed, hollow-eyed children whose rust-tinged hair suggests malnutrition. The open sewers emit a dizzying stench. Rats big as housecats skitter through piles of trash, and sweating, sinewy men crouch in shade where they can find it, their eyes bloodshot and hooded.

As I walk, soaking up the sparkling expanse of sea and the closer chaos of street commerce, I finally come across the traffic jam's source. A remarkable roadblock traverses the boulevard, rudely fashioned of tree limbs, piles of garbage, a broken bicycle, and, as its centerpiece, a dead body. The corpse is that of a middle-aged man. He is shirtless and shoeless. He wears pants, but the zipper is down and his genitals are exposed, as if they've been yanked from his pants. This weird tableau is what has brought traffic to a halt.

Haiti is the most mind-boggling place I know—a country where, as an American ambassador once said, you can believe nothing of what you hear and only half of what you see. I crisscross the country on repeated trips, driving on dried-up riverbeds to follow rumors of massacres, covering coups d'état so frequent they might be thunderstorms, writing about the competing epidemics of AIDS, boat people, deforestation, corruption, hunger.

Amid all this misery, there is a tiny, French-speaking elite that enjoys a tight grip on the relatively few profit-making enterprises in the country. At the American embassy, these oligarchs are referred to as MREs—"morally repugnant elites." They drive Land Rovers, reside in palatial villas, and have second homes in Miami and New York. In the cool, leafy precincts of Pétionville, which overlooks Port-au-Prince like a gargoyle, chic restaurants cater to them, and the food is terrific.

At one of the city's most fashionable places—dazzling white walls hung with tastefully framed paintings, tables draped with starched linen, a tempting menu of Creole specialities—the owner is notorious for her temper. She approaches me one evening, agitated that one of my colleagues, a correspondent from the *New York Times,* has portrayed the Haitian dictator of the moment as a bit of a thug. (I have too, but she has not seen my paper.) "The *salaud!*" she says, furious at the *Times* man. My French is good enough to know that Madame has just called my colleague a bastard.

"You know what I will do?" she says, shaking her big finger at me. I do not know, and say so. "The next time he comes in here, I will poison his pumpkin soup."

I laugh, and am promptly scolded by Madame.

"You don't think so? Just watch!"

Madame is formidable. She's built like a linebacker, and wears a dazzling white sleeveless dress. Her hair is encased in a brightly colored cloth, wrapped almost like a turban. She is a very good cook. Her pumpkin soup is renowned, and so is her *griot*—a traditional Haitian dish of crusty deep-fried cubes of pork, served with a vinegary sauce.

Madame's threat seems worth heeding. A few years earlier, a notorious chieftain of the Tontons Macoutes, the squadron of thugs used by the Duvalier dictatorship to terrorize the country, had died after eating a bowl of pumpkin soup. I pay for my dinner, thank Madame, and, on returning to the hotel, find my colleague from the *Times.* I recount Madame's threat and suggest that henceforth he avoid her pumpkin soup. He says he may avoid Madame's restaurant altogether.

My Haitian guide and translator, Patrick, has the height and build of a basketball forward. He is manic, charismatic, and good-looking. When I meet him, Patrick has just returned to Haiti after four years in New York, where he put himself through Columbia University by scalping tickets at Radio City Music Hall.

When I'm not around he hangs with a crew of Colombian cocaine traffickers for whom he serves, as far as I can tell, as a sort of courier. He wears a bullet on a golden chain around his neck, a pistol in his belt, and a thick wad of hundreds in a silver money clip in his pocket. Strictly speaking, I should not be working with Patrick, but I figure everyone in Haiti is corrupt in some way, and few have his talents.

These include a knack for talking his way into and out of practically anything. Once, intent on interviewing boat people preparing for their departure, we are surrounded on the beach by a group of men brandishing machetes who believe I am an American spy who would betray their plans to sail to Florida and seek asylum. (Except for the spy part, this is not far from the truth; I am, after all, in the business of writing about what I can learn.) The men back us into the surf up to our shins before Patrick unleashes such a tirade of electrifying oratory, by turns hectoring and hilarious, that the men back down, dissolving in laughter and accepting a peace offering of cigarettes.

A few months later, in the aftermath of a coup, we are in a slum courtyard interviewing a *vodoun* priest and his three wives, who are describing a murderous rampage by army troops. The priest has just returned to the neighborhood, which is otherwise deserted. We've been talking for ten minutes when two army jeeps screech up. They disgorge a dozen soldiers and their commander, a wild-eyed captain. The captain is apoplectic; the tendons on his neck are bulging. He is screaming, calling us "provocateurs"— the only word I can make out from his tirade in Creole—pointing his pistol in Patrick's face and then in mine, his finger on the trigger. His men prod us in the ribs with the muzzles of their M16s, enjoying my terror.

Patrick attempts to soothe the captain with a bribe and, failing that, calmly informs him that I am President Bush's personal emissary, a close friend of First Lady Barbara Bush, and—he throws this in for good measure—a former aide-de-camp to General Colin Powell, chairman of the Joint Chiefs of Staff.

He explains that any harm that befalls us will be taken as a grave insult by the White House and the Pentagon's top brass. For proof, Patrick tells me to produce my driver's license ("more official-looking than your press card," he explains later) and carefully pronounces "Washington, D.C." for the benefit of the captain, who is evidently illiterate. Drenched in sweat and still enraged, the captain nonetheless orders his men to withdraw, though not before shooting out the tires of Patrick's Land Rover and firing a few more shots from his pistol just over our heads.

When they are gone, Patrick shrugs. "In Haiti we are all little dictators," he says. "That captain, those soldiers, the president—even me!"

I leave Haiti feeling drained and stunned, as if I have dived into a swamp full of alligators and swum a dozen laps. At the Port-au-Prince airport, I run a gauntlet of pickpockets, begging children, and foreign travelers panicked by the terminal's routine pandemonium, and pay a series of small bribes at customs, though I am carrying nothing of any value. Once I clear passport control, I collapse in the departure lounge, drink Barbancourt rum, and chain-smoke cigarettes. I don't fully relax until the plane is wheels-up, bound for Miami.

In the hum of the flight over the Caribbean, I stare down at the clouds, my thoughts toggling from the soldiers and their wild-eyed captain to my grandparents. They expect to see me tonight for the early bird special at a new Vietnamese place in Boca. They're going with friends—"the Shermans from Brooklyn!" my grandmother tells me when I call—and they want to show me off. I think of the soldiers and their M16s and the *vodoun* priest. And I think it has been a hell of a trip—one unbelievable hell of a trip—and what I'd really like is to put off my grandparents for a day or two so I can be by myself tonight, at a spectacular Cuban restaurant I know in Coral Gables, and order every damn thing on the menu.

A DIET FOR DICTATORS

~NORTH KOREA~

BARBARA DEMICK

IN 2003, A JAPANESE SUSHI CHEF BEARING THE PSEUDONYM KENJI Fujimoto penned a memoir that gave rise to the expression "cook and tell." The subject of Fujimoto's indiscretion was Kim Jong Il, for whom he had served as personal chef for more than a decade. The rotund North Korean leader had greater passion for good food than for beautiful women, allowing his chef as intimate an understanding of his psyche as any of his many purported mistresses, though none of them—as far as I know—ever wrote a memoir.

Fujimoto was recruited in 1982 by a Japanese-Korean trading company to work at an elite restaurant in Pyongyang for five thousand dollars per month. Six years later, he was asked to be the personal cook for Kim Jong Il, then the heir-apparent to his father, North Korea's founder, Kim Il Sung. As Fujimoto tells it, he soon became a companion to the younger Kim. Both men were in their forties at the time. They went horseback riding, hunting, and jet-skiing together. They ogled dancing girls at banquets. But most of all, they obsessed about food. Fujimoto ingratiated himself with Kim through his superior knowledge of food. They talked recipes. Fujimoto regaled his patron with anecdotes from Japan's great kitchens and markets, especially Tokyo's Tsukiji fish market, where Fujimoto had spent six months learning how to fillet fish. He showed Kim videos of cooking shows that Fujimoto's sister had taped from Japanese television.

Although Kim was at the time renowned for his heft (only five feet two inches tall, he weighed more than two hundred pounds), the North Korean was a gourmet, not a glutton. He took food seriously and owned a collection of several thousand cookbooks. His palate was so sensitive that he could detect if the kitchen added a few grams too much sugar to the sushi rice. Before cooking the rice, the kitchen staff would inspect each grain individually and discard any blemished by irregularities of shape or color. He ate only the choicest foods and loved the fatty cut of tuna known as *toro*.

Sometimes Fujimoto would prepare sashimi using a trick he'd learned at Tsukiji, slicing so the vital organs were spared and the fish was served writhing on the platter. Kim loved shark's fin, a delicacy across Asia, and *poshintang*, a dog-meat soup that Koreans believe strengthens immunity and virility.

Money was no object when it came to food. Fujimoto made shopping trips around the world to pick up ingredients—to Iran and Uzbekistan for caviar, to Denmark for pork, to Thailand for mangoes, durians, and papayas. On a whim, Kim once sent Fujimoto to pick up a box of his favorite rice cakes, which were scented with mugwort and available only at a department store in Tokyo. Fujimoto later calculated the trip and put the cost of each bite-size morsel at $120.

Fujimoto worked for Kim until 2001, when he defected back to Japan, escaping on the pretext of making a shopping run to pick up *uni,* or sea urchin, to make a dish they'd seen on one of the videos. Since the publication of his first book, he has written two more about his time in North Korea. He makes frequent appearances on television, usually wearing aviator shades and a bandana to disguise his identity. I never got a chance to speak directly to Fujimoto (when I requested an interview shortly after the publication of his first book, I was told there would be a fee), but I have read excerpts of his writing translated into English and heard his views on issues ranging from denuclearization to the process for choosing a successor in North Korea. It is as though he peered through the gullet straight into the heart and soul of one of the world's most enigmatic leaders.

I don't mean to dismiss what Fujimoto writes. He is taken seriously by the intelligence community and by journalists like myself following North Korea. The chef is one of the few outsiders who has personally met Kim Jong Un, Kim's youngest son and heir-apparent. Indeed, Fujimoto gained some credibility by correctly picking out Jong Un, whom he'd met as a child, as the likely successor. "A chip off the old block, a spitting image of his father in terms of face, body shape and personality," he wrote in his first book. He also supplied the world with the first (and as of this writing in 2010, only) confirmed photograph of the successor.

Another account comes from Ermanno Furlanis, an Italian chef, who published a three-part series in the *Asia Times* titled "I Made Pizza for Kim Jong Il." The tell-all Italian chef, who worked in the private kitchens for a stint in 1997, never met the North Korean leader (Kim took over after his father's death in 1994), but got an up-close view of what he and others in his retinue were eating. "Every now and then a kind of courier would show up from some corner of the world. I saw him twice unloading two enormous boxes containing an assortment of 20 very costly French cheeses, and one box of prized French wines. That evening, dinner—a feast worthy of Petronius' *Satyricon*—was served with an excellent Burgundy and delicacies from around the world. As an Italian I could not refrain from objecting, and three days later fresh from Italy a shipment of Barolo arrived."

Yet another tale of excess comes from Konstantin Pulikovsky, a Russian official who accompanied Kim on a train trip through Russia in 2001 and turned the experience into a book called *Orient Express*. Pulikovsky says that fresh consignments of wine and live lobster were flown in at various stops along the way and that dinner typically consisted of fifteen to twenty dishes. Kim "would take only a little, as if to taste it," wrote Pulikovsky, who apparently spent much of the journey discussing gastronomy with Kim as well as procuring Russian delicacies. "You get the feeling that he knows what's what in culinary matters."

Of course, there is nothing wrong with being a foodie—except when you are the leader of a small, impoverished country where almost everybody else is eating grass. Most of the excesses described above took place during the famine of the 1990s, which killed off up to two million North Koreans, about 10 percent of the population. And the statistics about the death toll do not tell the full story. Those who survived—much of the current population—suffer from chronic malnutrition. A study by South Korean anthropologists of North Korean children who had defected to China found that eighteen-year-old males were five inches shorter than South Koreans their age. Roughly 45 percent of North Korean children under the age of five are stunted from malnutrition. It's impossible to calculate what percentage of the total food budget for twenty-two million people is squandered on this one person and his coterie of family and friends. In addition to his edibles, Kim is said to have a wine cellar with ten thousand fine bottles and, as has long been reported, to be the world's single largest customer of Hennessy's top cognac.

In fact, many serious analysts of North Korea have mined reports of Kim's eating habits for clues into the nature of the North Korean leader. The founder and former director of the CIA's Center for the Analysis of Personality and Political Behavior, Jerrold M. Post, in fact diagnosed Kim Jong as "a malign narcissist" in large part based on information about his eating habits. Kim "has this special sense of self so that there is no contradiction between the exquisite care that goes into his own cuisine and the fact that half his population is starving," Post told me in an interview shortly after Fujimoto's book was published. Post, who has also profiled Saddam Hussein and Osama bin Laden, was struck not only by the shamelessness with which Kim craved luxury, but also by his fussiness about how ordinary foods should be prepared. Not only was each grain of rice to be inspected but, according to a memoir by one of Kim's relatives, the rice had to be prepared the old-fashioned way over a wood fire using trees from Mount Paektu, a legendary peak straddling the Sino-Korean border that Kim claims (falsely) as his birthplace. Post suggested the elaborate preparation of the rice is in keeping with the ideological underpinnings of a system in which Kim and his father are treated as divine—more like the former cult of the Japanese emperor than a true communist regime. "This is how you prepare food and water for a god. Nothing remotely imperfect should cross his lips," said Post.

Yet one gets the feeling that Kim Jong Il, in his heart of hearts, knows that his people wouldn't be pleased if they knew what he spends feeding himself. North Korean propaganda often describes Kim as sharing the suffering of his people and living as they do. For his sixty-second birthday, one account carried by the official KCNA news service described Kim eating with soldiers he was visiting. "That evening, potato dishes were prepared for his simple dinner. . . . In this way, Kim Jong Il spent his birthday with devotion to the country and his people." The North Korean media often extol the virtues of eating with restraint, a convenient propaganda line in a country where food is always scarce. In the early 1990s, as famine first gripped the country, North Korean state television ran a documentary about a man whose stomach burst, it claimed, from eating too much rice. About the same time, billboards went up around Pyongyang with the slogan "Let's eat two meals a day!"

North Koreans are also instructed that they should eat only foods distributed by the government's public distribution system and that it is "antisocialist" to buy or sell staples like rice and corn on the market. As far as growing your own food is concerned, only the smallest "kitchen gardens" in backyards and on rooftops are legal. In recent years, Kim Jong Il's police have swept through markets, confiscated food, and arrested vendors who violate the rules, compounding the existing food shortages, since the government is unable to provide enough to sustain the population.

As for the foreign delicacies enjoyed by Kim Jong Il, North Koreans are instructed that they are to be avoided, like foreign clothing, hairstyles, music, and film, as symptoms of "rotten bourgeois ideology"—to use the language of a Workers' Party pamphlet somebody once gave me. "Make dishes that are familiar to the palate so our people's food is handed down to our descendants," instructed the pamphlet, which was dated from 2005 and distributed to party cadres. "Our people's food is refreshing and has a nice aroma. It stimulates good nutrition and protects your health."

For a country synonymous with famine, North Korea has a surprisingly sophisticated cuisine, distinct in the way it combines sour, sweet, spicy, and pungent ingredients to produce an effect that could best be described as "tangy." It is unlike anything else in Asia, and most Koreans I know, especially North Koreans, complain that Chinese food is too oily and Japanese food too sweet. The distinctive taste is encapsulated by *naeng myun*, the signature dish of Pyongyang—cold buckwheat noodles served in a vinegary broth with myriad regional variations, including hard-boiled eggs, cucumber, Asian pear, radish, or, in expensive restaurants, slivers of brisket. North Koreans are also good cooks, and many who defect to South Korea end up opening restaurants. Perhaps it is the years of scarcity that have honed their creativity in making tasty things to eat out of meager ingredients. A long history of famines has made Koreans expert in finding wild foods—pine mushrooms, seaweed, tiny clams—and turning them into delicacies. A seemingly endless variety of tasty herbs and greens (many of them lacking exact translations in English) are collected in the wild and served as delicious salads sprinkled with chiles and soy sauce. Schoolchildren are sent out to collect acorns, from which the nuts are extracted and pounded into a pulp to make a jelly known as *dotorimuk*. For the long winters without access to fresh vegetables, the North Korean diet relies heavily on *kimchi*, the spicy preserved cabbage that accompanies every meal. Unlike in South Korea and Korean restaurants abroad, where barbecued beef is the most popular dish, in North Korea it is generally not permitted to consume beef, except in small portions in soups or stews. It is more common to get pork, or sometimes goat, rabbit, or dog. But meat of any kind is rare, and most people get to eat it only on public holidays, namely, Kim Il Sung and Kim Jong Il's birthdays, when extra rations are distributed so as to remind North Koreans that all good things in their country result from the munificence of their leadership.

The real problem for North Koreans is the lack of rice. Rice is by far the preferred staple of North Korea—so much so that the word for meal is the same as for rice, *bap*. Kim Il Sung once promised that North Koreans would be able to eat rice every day ("Socialism is rice," he claimed), but the promise went unfulfilled. Rice, especially white rice, remains a luxury. Most people eat a hodgepodge of whatever grains are available, sometimes barley or corn, but not the way we know it. North Koreans will often throw the cobs and husks into the grinder to make the mixture go further.

Other so-called substitute foods include grass and leaves. Andrew S. Natsios, a former U.S. Agency for International Development administrator, described in a fine book he wrote in 2001 about the North Korean famine an instructional video obtained from North Korea in the 1990s that showed how to harvest pondweed, dry it out, and add it as an extender to wheat or corn flour for making noodles. "In one part of the tape, corn husks, oak leaves and grass are ground up into powder and passed through a noodle machine," Natsios wrote. "The resulting noodles have little nutritional value, cannot be digested by the human system, and in fact cause severe gastrointestinal problems for those hungry enough to eat them. . . . In my decade of involvement in famine relief efforts, I had never seen such a bizarre manifestation of a hunger coping mechanism as this videotape."

Other coping mechanisms are equally ineffectual. A doctor who defected from North Korea in 1998 said she used to advise patients to boil noodles for at least an hour to make them look bigger. During the 1990s, young people would climb pine trees to strip away the tender inner bark, which could also be dried out, ground, and used as a flour. Many North Korean defectors describe the degrading experience of looking for spilled grains of rice or corn on the ground, and it was not uncommon for those really hungry to extract undigested kernels of corn from animal excrement.

The North Koreans I've met are, like Kim Jong Il, obsessed with food. They wake up early worrying about what to eat for breakfast, spend their entire day trying to scrounge up something to eat for dinner. Lunch is a luxury. When the UN World Food Programme in 2008 conducted a survey of 250 North Korean households, they found the kitchens empty and most people unable to answer the question, What will you eat for your next meal? "They would give vague answers," recalled Jean-Pierre de Margerie, who was at the time heading the WFP office in Pyongyang. " 'I'm hoping my relatives who live on a cooperative farm will deliver some potatoes tonight.' "

One woman I know well was a garment factory worker, a mother of five and a talented amateur cook from Chongjin, a city in North Korea's far northeast. Before the famine, Song Hee-suk would make elaborate meals out of the food rations doled out by what is called the public distribution system. When there was rice, it would be soaked and then ground, to be turned into a dough to shape into cakes that could be served sweet or fried with chiles. Every autumn she made more than nine hundred pounds of kimchi in different varieties, with cabbages or radishes or turnips, seasoned with red pepper, bean paste, baby shrimp. Since meat was scarce, she learned dozens of methods to prepare tofu in soups or stews, or dried and fried—when there was no cooking oil, always scarce in North Korea, she figured out how to fry in soy sauce alone.

When almost everything else had run out and both she and her husband had lost their jobs, she made soup with only water and salt and a handful of the cheapest cornmeal, adding leaves and grass to make it appear as if the soup contained vegetables. She would wake up at 5:00 A.M. to rush out before her neighbors to find the freshest new growth of greens, knowing that tenderer weeds were easier to digest. Mrs. Song survived on little more than this basic diet for nearly a decade, though her husband and only son were not so lucky: they died of starvation in 1997 and 1998, respectively, around the same period that that Kim Jong Il's Italian chef was writing awestruck about the caseloads of expensive cheese arriving from France.

In 2002, Mrs. Song escaped from North Korea and made her way to South Korea, where she now lives. I met her two years later when I started researching a project about the lives of ordinary North Koreans. Since my newspaper's ethics rules forbid paying for interviews, I wanted to make sure that I at least treated North Korean defectors to a good meal during their interviews. Mrs. Song was an eager subject. She was in her own way a frustrated gourmet—while other North Koreans couldn't wait to surf the Internet or watch Hollywood movies, Mrs. Song's desire was to try new foods. We went to buffet restaurants where she could partake from the heaping platters of sushi, mounds of smoked salmon, white asparagus spears, mousses, pecan pies, and dainty tartlets of lemon meringue that were a revelation with each bite. Not that Mrs. Song ever stuffed herself. Like the other North Koreans I'd met, she was terrified when she first saw people who were obese—another revelation—and she always ate slowly, sparingly. I once took her to a French restaurant at the Chosun Hotel in Seoul, where she filled up on the bread basket (I didn't have the heart to tell her you're not expected to eat all the bread). When the filet mignon arrived, she looked at it with some trepidation—big slabs of beef are unheard of in North Korea—and left most of it unfinished on the plate. We had a happier experience when we went back to Korean food, heading with two of her grandchildren and her son-in-law to a restaurant in Suwon, a city south of Seoul famous for its *kalbi*, barbecued beef ribs. We settled into a booth and the waitress brought out the meat, marinated in soy sauce and sesame oil, and grilled it on a charcoal fire on our table before cutting it off the bone with a pair of scissors. We ate it wrapped in lettuce leaves with bean paste and nibbled from the side dishes—a cold, raw crab in spicy sauce, a sweet radish kimchi, potato salad—and then washed it down with two bottles of a Chilean Cabernet Sauvignon. I don't think Kim Jong Il ever enjoyed a meal as much.

SIEGE FOOD

~BOSNIA~

JANINE DI GIOVANNI

PAUL, THE FRENCH RADIO JOURNALIST WHO WORE SHINY CITY SHOES in the grimy snow, and a big black wool topcoat instead of a flak jacket with plates, looked up from his dinner: "My grandfather in Buchenwald," he said somberly, "ate better than this."

It was ten days before Christmas, Sarajevo, 1992, the first year of a nasty and terrifying war. I was sitting in the Holiday Inn at a dinner table covered by a dirty white cloth, with three other people.

There was Paul; there was Joel—a handsome surfer kid from California who arrived improbably on a Eurail Pass at the beginning of the siege and ended up staying throughout, eventually becoming a star reporter—and there was Kurt from Reuters. Joel and I were sitting at the table in our flak jackets, which is what we did in those days—the shells came very close to the hotel, and besides, they kept you warm.

On that freezing-cold winter night in wartime Sarajevo, our meal was not delicious and there was no alcohol. Our dinner consisted of half a plate of boiled rice, congealed and slightly burned, a pile of what looked like delicate bird bones in one corner of the plate. The entire concoction was covered in a lumpy paste that was meant to be brown gravy.

Kurt, who was vegetarian, pushed the plate away, and Paul muttered deep disgust in French. But Joel and I, American kids who grew up hearing stories about children starving in Biafra, ate slowly, spooning the burned rice into our mouths until the plates were clean. There was no chance of getting any more food until morning, which was a long way off.

I was the new kid there, freshly arrived from central Bosnia, so I wasn't sure how much complaining I could do without appearing spoiled. It was my first real war. I had had stones thrown at me in the West Bank and had met with militants on the run in Gaza, but nothing was quite like Bosnia. When we came out the back door of the Holiday Inn, there were snipers watching us who could easily aim at our kneecaps.

And you never knew when a shell was going to come crashing down, sending hot shrapnel flying and decimating everything in its path. You weren't even safe inside. I knew someone whose mother stayed in for the entire siege but was killed by shrapnel that flew through her window as she was washing dishes the last year of the war. Sarajevo was like a doll's house, someone once said, with a giant poised above it throwing rocks below at whatever took his fancy.

It may have been hard to stomach, but what we were eating at the Holiday Inn, the wartime dormitory for journalists smack in the middle of Sniper's Alley, was Julia Child's *canard à l'orange* compared to what was available in the city outside our door. There, the civilian population of Sarajevo was subsisting on rice, macaroni, cooking oil, a small packet of sugar, and some tinned meat or fish. This came out of a humanitarian aid package that arrived, if they were lucky, every few weeks.

"Imagine what it is like to be eternally dependent on someone else for what is put in your mouth," Mario, a Bosnian poet friend, said to me. "Imagine that you have no rights anymore, even to eat."

I did not yet know how crazy people would get for a piece of meat, or the hot drag of a real cigarette—a Marlboro Red, for instance. In fact, a man had positioned himself near the Holiday Inn selling puffs of a cigarette for a few deutsche marks each.

Meals at the Holiday Inn, though spare, were attempts to be classy. The food came on thick white ceramic plates, the tables were lit by candles—because there was no electricity, not to create a romantic ambience—and the waiters wore clean white shirts and black or green vests with little bow ties. The candlelight helped the food situation: once you put some salt—if there was some—on the rice, it was masked and you did not know what you were eating. It was simply something grainy and salty. The BBC brought bottles of Tabasco, so all you tasted was your tongue on fire.

That night, Kurt asked for some cheese. At breakfast, along with the hard bread made from sawdust and water, there was sometimes a home-made cream paste, which we suspected was made from cooking oil and ground rice. (Breakfast was always depressing, as you climbed out of your sleeping bag cold and went to the dining room cold, yearning for coffee but getting boiled water. Once at breakfast, a few months later, I would see writer Susan Sontag squirreling away a sack of bread to give to her starving actors, whom she was directing in *Waiting for Godot*. Her actors, not surprisingly, adored her.)

"There is nothing else tonight," Said, one of my favorite waiters, told Kurt. "I am so sorry." It wasn't a surly response. It was the truth. There was never anything else, or anything worth eating. As for alcohol, you had to supply your own on trips back to Western Europe or to Zagreb or Split. The wine cellar of the restaurant, which apparently had not been bad for an Eastern European capital, had been drained dry by journalists the summer before. But we were not there for the cuisine, and we got used to it.

The Holiday Inn was a testament to resilience. It should have been blown off the map, but it survived numerous attacks. The toilets did not flush and there was no running water—at one point during the summer of 1993, there was a cholera scare and we had to drop funny red pills into the carafes of water—but still, we were lucky. Everything we ate, every ounce of oil that sparked our generators came from the black market. We paid handsomely to live in that third-rate university dormitory and someone, somewhere was making a huge profit.

"Baklava!" I will never forget the joy on the face of Chris, a Reuters photographer, when he saw the "dessert" one night. In fact, it tasted nothing like the sublime honey-coated flaky pastry I have eaten in Beirut or Athens; but it was an attempt at normalcy. Normalcy was important. Everyone tried to maintain their balance. The Sarajevo girls still put on lipstick and dyed their hair with lye during the siege, because they refused to be frumpy. "If that happens," said one friend who applied her eyeliner as the bombs crashed down, "the Serbs have won the war. We must, we *must* be normal."

Food is always a precious commodity in a city under siege. In Sarajevo, everything could be bought and sold for a Mars Bar. And we were lucky. Because we were journalists, and therefore had cash and access to things the people of Sarajevo did not, we could manage far better than the local populace. Système D, the French *journos* called it—the World War II strategy of making do—how to make the best when you have nothing in your hands.

That's when I first noticed the national differences among the reporters. Next to our foursome that night was a French TV crew—Antenne 2, I think—who were feasting. They had brought bottles of Burgundy, *saucisses,* slabs of cheese. They were aided by the *Libération* reporter Didier François, who was slicing the *saucisses* with a Swiss army knife, and Ariane, a mouthy little freelancer who drove a German armored car so huge she could barely see over the steering wheel. On her head, during dinner, was a Russian fur hat, and she was happily chewing on a fatty piece of sausage. (Some months later, during a break from Sarajevo, we met for lunch at La Coupole in Paris, and I saw the same joy on her face as she ordered their famous AAA *andouillette* sausage. "Truck driver food!" she said happily.)

They were always generous, the French, but at some point people looked after themselves. Even if someone offered you a piece of sausage, you probably would have to refuse it out of politeness. You could take it once, but the second time, no way. The Italian journalists were the most reliable. They usually arrived in Sarajevo with enormous wedges of Parmesan or pecorino cheese and asked the waiters to cook pasta, which they brought in by the sack.

They would cook up a huge bowlful, and the waiters would bring it to their table with a flourish, and then one of the Italians would dish it out to everyone on little plates. The entire dining room got a taste. It reminded me, in the middle of the intense loneliness that was Sarajevo, of lunches at my Italian grandfather's house when I was a child. There was something immensely comforting about seeing them gathered around that steaming bowl of spaghetti.

The Brits brought chocolate—the *Observer* reporter once came to my room with a huge bag of Maltesers and mini Bounty bars, and we ate them all on Saturday waiting for our reports to be cleared by our desks back in London.

The Americans, as a rule, did not share. The big guns from CNN sat grandly by themselves in a corner, ignoring peons like us. American newspaper reporters tended to operate like lone wolves: each man for himself. I remember one reporter coming down to breakfast with two eggs in his pocket. He removed them and asked the waiter to cook them. He did this in front of the rest of us, who probably had not tasted an egg for some time. But what the hell! It was war. Shamelessly he ate the fried eggs, dipping hard bread into the yolk.

Reporters from other networks, like ABC and NBC, were much kinder, especially if you were poor and a freelancer; and later, when the summer came, a kind producer named Carlo based in Split would send in boxes of fresh tomatoes that he grew in his gardens, along with heads of garlic and onions. By then, with the siege still going strong, people were exhausted. I had forgotten what a salad, what a peach was. I had huge spontaneous bruises all over my body. When I went to London, my doctor did a blood test and my anemia was so severe that he made me carry bottles of a putrid German tonic called Floradix back to Sarajevo with me.

Once, I am embarrassed and horrified to admit, when I had a terrible hangover I paid twenty-five marks for a can of Coca-Cola on the black market. Coca-Cola, a Croatian journalist called Sasa told me, could sustain you for more than a month in case you were pinned down, for example, in Vukovar or the eastern side of Mostar. "Sugar, water, caffeine," he said, and I believed him. "You'll stay alive, at least."

After a while, this is all food was to us: a way of staying alive and putting energy into our bodies. At a certain point, I gave up and lived on Toblerone bars. To this day, I cannot look at Toblerone bars. And I smoked and smoked, which helped, and all of us drank an awful lot. Alcohol drowned out everything, most of all the terrible things that were happening outside, which will haunt me for the rest of my life.

Outside the Holiday Inn that night ten days before Christmas was the war, but it was also snowing, big fat snowflakes coming down quietly between the heavy thumping of the shells.

There were no Christmas trees in Sarajevo for the Catholics celebrating the holiday that year: they had all been chopped down for firewood. Instead, there was a yellow fog in Sarajevo, a cold winter fog. The cold went right through your bones, which was unfortunate because there was no heating anywhere, and the few places in the city that still operated—a bakery, for instance, where you could occasionally get bread—meant you had to wait in huge long lines. For hours people stood in the cold, until they no longer felt their legs.

At the beer factory on the other side of the river, you could get water. People lined up with buckets, standing there as well for hours in their gloves and hats and warm coats, blowing on their fingers and stamping their feet to stay warm.

On winter mornings before Christmas I walked through Veliki Park. There were old people dragging twigs on sleds, small children sliding on the ice. Then came the crackle of a sniper rifle somewhere not so far from us, maybe five hundred yards away. Everyone froze, and then scurried away.

About this time I met a lovely but sad girl. Klea lived on top of a hill, Bjelave, in a tiny little house set back in a tiny garden with her husband, Zorky, and her tiny baby, Deni. The daughter of a professor of English— Mario, the poet—she had spent part of her life in America and England and was named after the character in Durrell's *Alexandria Quartet*. Her little sister, in fact, was called Alexandra.

The war had started when Klea was pushing Deni in his baby carriage in April the spring before, and she was not happy being a first-time mother and a young wife in a city with shells crashing around her. Still, she was resilient and went about her days with a faint air of defiance and a large cloud of melancholy. She was delicate and birdlike, and pretty, with dark hair and enormous blue eyes inherited from her mother, Marija, who was equally melancholy. It was no fun to be young and pretty in Sarajevo during the war.

Klea coped pretty well with the nightmare around her—the snipers positioned on the hills around the city when she went to stand in her lines; her father, Mario, quietly losing his mind and burning all his books to keep warm; being unable to feed the beloved dog; seeing the apocalyptic scenes on the street. It was hard to feed Deni properly, to get him milk. The child got only the powdered variety, but it appeared not to affect him—he was flourishing despite the siege. And Klea refused to let the Serbs get to her.

Klea was a Catholic Croat, but like most people in Sarajevo before the war, she and Zorky were a mixed couple—Zorky was part Serb, part something else no one thought to inquire about before the war. Muslims celebrated Christmas. Catholics celebrated Bajram. Jewish friends celebrated everything. There seemed to be no ethnic divisions. And Klea wanted to celebrate Christmas.

"So what are we going to make for Christmas dinner?" She stood in front of me, pretty and tired, her jeans sagging on her body, which was emaciated. A week before, she had been standing in a line waiting for bread and a sniper's bullet went right through her jeans. It left an entry and exit mark but missed her flesh because she had lost so much weight.

Klea wanted *borek* for Christmas, the traditional Bosnian pie made with a flaky pastry and chopped meat and onions. You can also make it with spinach and cheese—like a Greek spanakopita. This is the Bosnian national dish, along with *cevapcici,* a greasy but delicious sausage sandwich that you eat with a glass of yogurt on the side. But *borek* is to Bosnians what pasta is to Italians. Every Bosnian mother has her own secret ingredient. In normal times, this is how you would make it:

Bosnian *Borek*

PASTRY
500 grams (about 1 pound) flour
25 grams (about 1 ounce or 2 tablespoons) butter
salt
water

FILLING
500 grams (about 1 pound) minced veal
250 grams (about 8 ounces) ground beef
4 onions
2 egg yolks
25 grams (about 1 ounce or 2 tablespoons) butter

Combine the pastry ingredients; roll out the dough and cut into four pieces. Mix together the veal, beef, onions, and egg yolks. Spread the filling over the pastry and roll up like a fat sausage. Brush with melted butter. Bake. Serve with double cream (whipping cream).

But this was not normal times. So Klea hoarded her dried eggs from her aid package for a few months and swapped them for a tin of humanitarian aid pork from her Muslim neighbor. "Disgusting," she said. But she made the

borek, and we all ate it that Christmas by candlelight with my contribution—
Toblerone bars, of course.

Klea had other recipes that had come from desperation. She would make
lepinja, the local equivalent of pita bread, which was traditionally made
with flour, oil, yeast, salt or sugar, powered milk, and water. She showed
me how she made cheese—a cup of powdered milk, a cup of oil, a cup of
water, salt, and a few drops of vinegar—or a faux Nutella spread from flour,
powdered milk, oil, cocoa, and sugar. (The amount of each ingredient
would be the same, depending on how much you had to start with. Mix all
together and cook for a few minutes.)

Greens would be supplemented by nettle. "It was a type of weed," she
remembers. "It stung your skin, like poison ivy when you touched it. We
boiled it and cut it and served it with rice." Salad was made from dandeli-
ons. "And if I had a potato, or some kind of meat," Klea says, "we mixed it
with whatever packaged food came from the humanitarian aid box." The
best, she says, was chicken à la king.

Bosnians love coffee. Every home I went to during the siege, no matter
how desperate, would serve coffee, Turkish style, cooked over a flame
with several teaspoons of sugar. It would be insulting to refuse it, and from
that time on I have been unable to drink weak coffee. Wartime coffee was
something else, though: it was made from rice that was roasted and then
ground.

The funny thing is, considering how desperately hungry and frightened
everyone was, a friend of mine called Lucky told me that surveys done during
the war showed that people were incredibly healthy. "I was as healthy as an
ox," he told me. People had great sex. The birth rate was up. Perhaps because
everyone lived on adrenaline, their immune systems managed to hold on.

It was only afterward that the survivors collapsed.

Klea and her family live in Canada now. They are Canadians, not Bosnians.
I have not seen Klea in sixteen years, but because of what we went through

together during those war years, we are still very close. Sisters, almost. She knows things about me I do not tell close friends. The war bonded us inseparably, forever. And I feel, I suppose thanks to e-mail and now Facebook, that I have seen her every day of all those years, war and postwar. Deni was too young when they left to remember much, certainly not the wartime food. But his mother does. Those years of scarcity are embedded in her memory.

I go back to Sarajevo often now, and once I went to the Holiday Inn. I actually stayed in the horrible place, which was empty, and saw some of the waiters. "Remember the soccer games that you had in the dining room at night? Because you could not go outside to play because of the snipers?" I asked. Said was not there, but the others pretended to remember. "Yes, yes, the war. Terrible days, the war."

I am looking back at that time from eighteen years' distance. I remember Paul, young and strange and handsome, not yet writing his novels, smoking a cigar. And I see his end by his own hand in a Parisian flat, after a tortured life. I see Kurt and me eating another dinner years later at a different table, one overlooking water in Freetown, Sierra Leone. We're eating prawns and salad and beer. The morning after, Kurt went down the road to a place called Rogberi Junction, where he got ambushed by some kids with RPGs and guns and never came back, not alive. And I think of Joel, who went to California, married, had children, continued to surf, and lives, I believe, a very happy life. He quit the war thing. I kept going for a while—too long, it seems.

It was a particularly nostalgic time of my life, that trip back. I stayed in my old room on the fourth floor. It's always a bad idea to go back in time and try to replicate a memory. Strangely, although the hotel was expensive, it had not changed much since the war—same awful purple and orange interiors and nasty fake wood furniture. I think they had changed the bedspreads—but we used sleeping bags anyway back in those days. And of course, the big difference was that the toilets flushed and there was running water for bathing.

They had moved the dining room to the back of the hotel. That would have been impossible during the war because it was the side of the building that got hit all the time. I ate fried eggs and toast, and drank cappuccino. No one remembered the red juice we had drunk at the beginning of the war—was it blackcurrant or cranberry? I went back to my room and packed my bag. Passing Kurt's old room, and Ariane's and Paul's, I mourned our younger selves. Too many ghosts. I picked up my case and left, and never stayed there again.

MIRACULOUS HARVESTS

~CHINA~

ISABEL HILTON

IT WAS MARC, A FRENCHMAN, WHO INSISTED WE EAT DOG MEAT. Marc was one of the more intrepid gastronomes in the small foreign student body in Beijing in 1974. Once he had found a place that served it, nobody could back out. Twelve of us went one evening. The dog was served in a rich brown stew, strong and slightly sweet. Childhood memories of dog breath discouraged me from repeating the experience.

The dog meal was one stop in a two-year journey through the byways of Chinese cuisine that began in Beijing in the autumn of 1973. It had started inauspiciously.

The first meal I ate in the People's Republic was served in the cavernous dining hall of the Beijing Languages Institute, at that time the only institute of tertiary education allowed to admit foreigners. China was closed, remote, and suspicious of Western visitors. It was a country full of secrets. A quarrel with Moscow had closed Soviet airspace to flights heading for Beijing, so travelers from Europe were obliged to take the long route across the Middle East to Pakistan before heading north across the Himalaya. It took nineteen hours to reach Beijing.

Ours was the only international flight to land that evening at Beijing's airport, and we were greeted by a British diplomat, several uniformed border guards, and a Chinese doctor in an oversize white coat who personified the government's view that foreigners brought dangerous contagion into the motherland. He offered a physical examination and threatened several injections. Behind the doctor, other servants of the Chinese revolution waited, alert to the dangers of infection from the cultural and political pathogens carried by the arriving foreigners.

A long bus ride through deserted city streets brought us to the institute's campus in northwestern Beijing. A giant statue of Chairman Mao dominated the front gate, gazing out across the quiet suburban street to the gates of the college opposite. The campus, like the rest of Beijing, seemed eerily quiet.

The officials who received us had given some thought to what these exotic new additions to the student body would eat. The meal, which appeared through a narrow hatch and was eaten in one corner of the chilly canteen, consisted of a gray fried egg, three slices of strangely sweet white bread, and a tall glass of sugared, milky tea. It represented the school authorities' idea of the debased culinary taste of the West, and no matter how disgusting they found it, they were unshakable in their conviction that we would prefer it to any local offering. Since Chinese could not be expected to eat unfamiliar food, they reasoned, foreigners must feel the same profound, if misguided, attachment to their own cuisine. In eating habits, as with other arrangements in Mao's China, apartheid was the rule.

Those were austere times. Beijing was dimly lit and subdued, the capital of a nation turned in on itself, its people wary that the wrong word or gesture could trigger devastating political consequences. They rose early and vanished from the streets as dusk fell, as though the rhythms of peasant life had infected the capital. They mimed their participation in the daily rituals of political campaigns; they seemed passive and drained of energy. Their curiosity about us, these aliens who had appeared in their midst, was expressed in mute staring. They would tug at their children's hands as we passed. If we stopped, they would encircle us, bemused by our odd clothes, the outlandish color of our hair, our large noses, our enviable leather shoes. If we tried to talk to them, they would stare us down or shuffle away.

The wide city streets were empty of cars except for the occasional official vehicle, its windows curtained to screen the occupants from the street. Freezing winds blew in from the Gobi Desert, carrying a stinging load of dust that sandblasted our faces and seeped through the badly fitted windows of the dormitory. We joined the monochrome drifts of cyclists pedaling slowly along the flat boulevards, skirting occasional camels and frequent mule carts, their drivers dozing on top of tottering loads. The streetlights were dim and the entire town was shuttered by 9:00 P.M. There were no bars or cafés, no nightclubs or discotheques. Cultural life was limited to the handful of films and revolutionary operas deemed politically pure.

For the visitor, Beijing was a closed city in which every foreigner who was not Albanian was a potential spy. There was no telephone directory and no guide to the city's many cultural landmarks. A few tourist attractions were open, but most of Beijing's temples had been destroyed, boarded up, or converted to other uses at the beginning of the Cultural Revolution, six years before. Precious statues had been smashed and rare books and paintings burned in an orgy of rage against the past. The great city walls had been pulled down to create a ring road on which few cars ever traveled. Exploration of the city was discouraged. Foreigners would be told what they needed to know; everything else—including news from outside China— was considered a secret not to be shared.

We were surrounded by people in the world's most populous country, but a wall of politics separated us from them. The Chinese students were polite, but conversation was limited to a nervous exchange of banalities. Only a few years earlier, any contact with foreigners had been enough to bring down the fury of the Red Guards and charges of treason. Nobody had forgotten the risks, and we were marooned in a virtual isolation ward of political disapproval. Those around us spent hours in political meetings from which we were excluded; when they were not studying the latest party instructions, they bent over their books or disappeared for long stints working in factories and on communes. The prospect of a year without social contact stretched out before us.

Exploring the rich traditions of Chinese food, we realized, was one of the few recreational possibilities available to us. It also provided the collateral benefit that we could at least share some public space with the local people, whose passion for their own cuisine seemed to have survived even the onslaught of the Maoist revolution. For us, this was a welcome diversion from the bleakness of institutional life. It was only afterward that I fully understood the gulf that separated our recreational indulgence from the preoccupations of the Chinese diners who crowded into the capital's restaurants.

Between 1960 and 1962, just over a decade earlier, an unknown number of Chinese had starved to death in what the official record still insists was a three-year stretch of natural disaster. The estimates of the dead vary from 30 million to 80 million. Every adult I encountered back then was a survivor of the worst mass starvation in human history.

It was a disaster created by politics. In 1958 Mao Zedong, in one of his periodic bouts of reckless hubris, launched China on a course of hectic industrialization that he boasted would bring China's steel-making capacity up to that of Britain within fifteen years. It was to be done through the collective efforts of the laboring masses, armed with the magic power of his own thought.

Hundreds of millions of peasants were organized into communes, their possessions—animals, land, and household goods—redesignated collective property overnight. They were to labor at the party's direction and be paid in kind through the distribution of the annual surplus, if surplus there was, according to how many work points they had earned in the course of the year. On top of their labor in the fields, they "voluntarily" dug irrigation ditches and steep hillside terraces, built roads and dams—many of which were to collapse—and, in fulfillment of Mao's steel-making ambitions, attempted to forge steel in makeshift backyard furnaces. Millions of people wasted months of effort and untold tons of fuel creating unusable pig iron.

The magic of Mao's thoughts extended to agriculture: the peasants must throw off their old conservative habits and harness themselves to the power of revolution. He ordered the grasslands ploughed up for wheat, grain to be planted more densely, rice to be grown where it had never been cultivated before. If his instructions were followed to the letter, he said, China's harvests would triple.

It went wrong from the beginning, but who would dare to tell him? To deny the magic was to betray the revolution, and what local official would volunteer for the disgrace of being designated a counterrevolutionary and the likelihood of a slow death in a labor camp? If the chairman ordained that they could triple the grain harvest, that is what would happen. From across China miraculous harvests were reported, yields abundant enough to fill the state granaries to capacity and still leave plenty for export.

But the magic of Mao's thought worked only in the minds of party faithful. In the peasants' fields, the harvests had collapsed; the thin topsoil of the ploughed-up grasslands had blown away, exposing barren rock; the closely planted grain had shriveled and died. The rice had withered in strange latitudes. Peasants had salvaged what they could, enough perhaps to see them through a lean winter and to give them some seed stock for the following year—provided no grain tax was collected.

When the magic of Mao's thought met the desperate reality of the countryside, the result was disaster. The grain tax was set high, in accordance with the miraculous harvests reported from across the country. When the peasants refused to pay it, they were accused of sabotaging the revolution and hoarding grain. State officials seized all they could find. Within a few months people began to go hungry, then to starve. By the time the policy was reversed—and Mao himself sidelined—the manmade famine had raged for three years.

Fifty years later, the government still prefers to blame the weather. Today, in a country of expanding waistlines, young people are bewildered by rumors of hunger in their parents' and grandparents' lives. But back in the 1970s, everyone remembered the desperation of just a decade before. Hungry ghosts still thronged the memories of the people we passed in the streets, and a bowl of rice was something that few of the living took for granted.

There was food, though it was not abundant. Grain, oil, and meat were all rationed, and restaurants required their customers to supply coupons for their meals. The coupons tied people to their home district; they were not valid elsewhere. Scarcity was still the rule. The campus canteen served compacted cubes of stale rice with bowls of thin vegetables. In the Beijing winter, great pyramids of cabbages appeared on the edge of the institute's playing fields, their bulk slowly dissipating as the cooks loaded wheelbarrows with tired cabbages to haul off to the canteen. Bright red persimmons were left outside to freeze and passed for ice cream. To buy an orange required a medical certificate. But in the parallel reality that foreigners occupied there were no grain coupons, perhaps to maintain the fiction of socialist abundance. We were free to eat where we chose.

For us, eating our way through China's gastronomic encyclopedia was an escape from the drab hostility of Mao's China. It was the only visible trace of the China of my imagination, the China that had first impelled me to climb the steep foothills of the language. I had landed in Beijing just as China's richly layered imperial past was in retreat. The Tang poetry that I wanted to study, the celadon glazes and gilded, curved roofs that I admired, the shaded courtyards hidden behind high gray walls that I longed to explore were all beyond reach. Traditional culture was banned as reactionary and all beliefs, other than socialism, condemned as superstition.

The culture of food, though, had stubbornly survived, albeit behind a facade of austere proletarianism. Restaurants were dilapidated and poorly lit, and their clients spat chewed debris freely onto the table or the floor. But behind the kitchen door, old skills had quietly been preserved, waiting for better times.

In the 1980s Mao's lifelong rival, the diminutive political survivor Deng Xiaoping, began to dismantle the dead chairman's legacy in earnest. He had suffered political disgrace twice, and on his third return to power he was a man in a hurry. The reforms he launched would set China on a path of headlong growth that would extinguish Maoist fundamentalism forever. Mao was reduced to the status of revered ancestor as the society that he had transformed into a socialist state turned to the market with enthusiasm.

By the 1990s, peasants had their collectivized land back under household control, though many would lose it again to rapacious local officials. The managers of state-owned factories operating at a loss abandoned the Maoist idea that everyone should have a job, and the factory workers discovered that there was a dark side to the market economy: they were no longer the proletarian elite, and their safe factory jobs evaporated. The managers grabbed large shareholdings in the new, slimmed-down enterprises, and the workers were left to fend for themselves.

As the People's Communes were broken up and the state factories dismantled, setting up in business became the lifeline of the newly redundant. Workers began to revive the skills of petty enterprise, and food production ceased to be a state monopoly. For some, it became a means of survival; for a few, it was the route to riches.

In Chongqing, a sweltering metropolis on the edge of the Yangtze River in Sichuan, former Red Guard Zhou Wenli and his wife set up a tiny hot pot restaurant. They began with a couple of tables on the pavement outside the family home. In a country in which innovation was still rare and where it was still considered dangerous to be different, one simple invention was to make the Zhous suddenly and fabulously rich. It was a gas-fired hot pot that was set into the table and divided in two sections; one was filled with a fiery, chile-laced version of the local dish, while the other side was blander.

It became a sensation. Within five years, the Zhous commanded a chain of large and lavish hot pot restaurants in ever-smarter locations. They added a cabaret of brightly dressed dancers, mostly peasant girls from mountain villages, in tinsel costumes. The colors were electric, as though the Zhous and their customers needed to erase the memory of two decades of mono-chrome living.

The restaurant chain did not just make the Zhous rich, it allowed them to retell the story of their lives. Mr. Zhou acquired a white Cadillac and a chauf-feur and dressed in tailored Western suits. The couple bought a generous detached house on a raw new estate. On their bedroom wall they hung their wedding photographs—not photographs of the day they had actually mar-ried, but photographs of the wedding they now felt they should have had.

Fifteen years earlier, their marriage had been a low-key affair, in line with the politics of the day. Nobody had dressed up, and the only treats were a handful of sweets and a few cigarettes shared with the local party offi-cials. It had been commemorated in a black-and-white photograph of the couple taken in front of a standard-issue poster of Chairman Mao. They stood staring at the camera, side by side, neither smiling nor touching.

The couple's talent for business had allowed them to leave those days far behind, but even their new affluence was not enough to make up for a youth lived in drab austerity. They had the power to carry their wealth into the fu-ture, but they also had the capacity to project it into the past, replacing their black-and-white memories with a colorful fantasy biography. They retroac-tively created the life that politics had denied them, a made-to-order life story in which they played the starring roles.

On the bedroom wall of their new villa, the utilitarian image of their socialist wedding was replaced with blown-up photographs of a wedding that never was. Mr. Zhou, dressed in a morning suit and top hat, leans to-ward the camera over the head of his wife, his gaze mimicking in its inten-sity that of the romantic lead in a Hollywood B movie. His bride is encased in an entire sweet shop of silk and lace, her heavily made-up face framed by a sculpture of black curls, topped with a white veil. The couple gazes out of the frame with the self-absorption of a pair of actors impersonating themselves for an admiring public.

The Zhous were not the only people who were rewriting their life story. The restaurants they opened were both places to eat and an invitation to share a fantasy of affordable glamour. Food was no longer about survival: across the country it was being reinvented to reflect a different China, a country that was suddenly turning out cheap goods for credit-fueled Western consumers and which, after years of isolation, was hungry to open to the world.

Ten years ago, a small street in central Beijing that I know well was a quiet, unpaved lane that boasted a greengrocer, a dry cleaner, and a small noodle shop. Now it offers thirty different restaurants, from Indian through Italian to Tibetan. A pair of elderly sisters have opened a tea shop in their living room and dispense homemade sponge cakes and apple tarts. A downmarket hotel sells lasagna and chili con carne to passing backpackers. Coffee, which few Chinese used to find palatable—one Chinese teacher once told me it tasted like medicine—is now so ubiquitous that Chinese friends think nothing of spending the equivalent of half a migrant worker's daily wage on a single Starbucks cappuccino. Tea drinking, too, has become a gourmet pursuit: an artist friend, known in the 1990s for his risqué performance art, recently chose to rendezvous at a teahouse where the brew he selected from the heavily brocaded menu cost thirty pounds for each tiny cup.

A dairy industry has sprung from nowhere in a country where cheese was once regarded with bewilderment and disgust, and exotic fruits and vegetables are on sale year-round. Kentucky Fried Chicken is now rumored to be China's biggest restaurant chain, and every city is infested with McDonald's. Meat eating, once a New Year's treat for many, has made young generations taller, while diabetes, obesity, and other afflictions of plenty are taking hold.

The Chinese people have never been so numerous or so well-off, and most can eat their fill, thanks to the thirty years of industrialization and economic growth. Hunger is a remote memory for the newly affluent in China's cities, but food remains at the center of the sense of well-being. Where once it was hoarded and husbanded, now it is dispensed with lavish extravagance. Wasting food is no longer seen as a sin against the labor of the peasant farmer but as a sign of lavish generosity in a wealthy host; in the competition for face, no animal is too exotic to end its days on the dining table. The rarer the creature, the more it boosts the host's reputation for good living. Poachers comb the forests and hills of neighboring countries for owls, crocodiles, pangolins, and civet cats to serve on China's tables. China's zoos offer visitors the opportunity, for a price, to eat the inmates, and the guardians of China's nature preserves have been known to celebrate important occasions by serving endangered species to their guests.

Old superstitions—that eating the corresponding part of an animal will cure an afflicted human organ—drive some of this traffic. In its most banal form, men eat animal penises in an effort to reassure themselves about the performance of their own. In a similar quest for potency, between 30 million and 100 million sharks are mutilated each year for the supposedly aphrodisiac qualities of their fins. Warnings that the elevated levels of mercury they contain might have the opposite physiological effect have not yet dented consumer demand. Nor has the suspicion that the Cantonese habit of eating civet cat contributed to the outbreak of SARS in 2002 had much impact on the popularity of the dish.

Prosperity has corroded China's memories of famine, but the industrial revolution has left a deadly deposit on the country's overloaded plates. In their race to produce, China's factories have left layers of contamination on soils and crops. The uncontrolled pollution that seeps from China's industrial centers dumps tons of toxins into the country's suffering rivers and renders long stretches of water unsafe to touch, let alone to drink. China's farmers still irrigate their crops, but now the water they use is laced with untreated sewage and industrial effluent that contains lead, arsenic, mercury, and other lethal heavy metals.

Beijing's winter cabbages now carry a load of cadmium and along the Yellow River, rice harvests are contaminated with chromium. The children who live along the riverbank appear to be suffering from sinister rates of mental retardation and stunted growth that doctors blame on high concentrations of arsenic and lead in their diet. And in China's fast-forwarded industrial revolution, which has allowed more people to eat more lavishly than ever before, food adulteration has become a national sport.

In the early years of this century, Chinese writer Zhou Qing, the kind of journalist that authoritarian governments regard as a dangerous nuisance, set out to investigate China's food industry. He discovered that Chinese farmers and food producers had embraced industrial innovation with enthusiasm, and the result was a catalog of horrors. Stories of an epidemic of early puberty in young children led him to investigate fish farms where the farmers had discovered that their fish grew faster if they were fed liberal quantities of contraceptive pills. He found that pork, another staple of the Chinese diet, was contaminated with clenbuterol, a drug that had been banned as an asthma treatment because of its dangerous side effects. China's farmers had discovered that it helped to produce lean meat in pigs, though those who ate the meat reported symptoms that included giddiness, nausea, and heart palpitations.

Soy sauce was being manufactured and exported in which fermented human hair, heavily contaminated with arsenic, was a major ingredient. Seafood was laced with formaldehyde and carcinogenic levels of a chemical called Malachite green that keeps fish scales looking fresh; eels were being killed with potassium permanganate before being shipped to market. Leather off-cuts from China's tanneries were being ground up to serve as animal and fish food. A Russian woman, Ilina Bulajina, caused a sensation when she reported finding drops of mercury in her oven after cooking some Chinese pork. The mercury, newspapers reported, had been injected to increase the weight.

Doctors began to attribute rising rates of cancer in Guangdong Province to the increased use of pesticides, additives, and preservatives. In one attention-grabbing speech, a scientist warned that sperm counts in the province had halved, despite the heavy consumption of alleged aphrodisiac foods. Diners were eating pesticide residues with their vegetables, sodium formaldehyde with their grains, and formaldehyde in their seafood.

If China's consumers were alarmed by reports of freak diseases or rumors of food-related cancer clusters, they had few alternatives in a market that valued rapid growth and discouraged the dissemination of bad news. Farmers, who knew what was going into their produce, admitted that they did not feed their own families the produce they sent to market. People in the cities, as one farmer told a reporter, had access to medical care, unlike poor farmers like himself.

Outside China, periodic scandals raised alarm about what horrors China's food concealed: European and U.S. inspectors chased down a periodic table of contaminants and residues in Chinese exports from seafood to honey, costing China hundreds of millions of dollars in lost revenue. Chinese diplomats and trade officials called foul and complained of discrimination, but back home officials were grappling unsuccessfully with the impossibility of maintaining safety in a system that lacked the key instruments of enforcement—the rule of law, consumer rights, a free press, and political accountability. China's full stomachs were important symbols of the success of the Communist Party's policies since the death of Mao; to suggest that what was filling those stomachs was less than wholesome was not just unwelcome, it bordered on unpatriotic.

In 2008, the toxic underworld of China's food industry and the Communist Party's propaganda machine collided in a spectacular scandal that threatened to wreck the party's most important moment in the international spotlight for thirty years. For a decade the nation had been mobilizing for a global demonstration of the transformational miracle of the previous thirty years: the 2008 Olympic Games, symbol of China's new importance in the world, were meticulously planned to be the most lavish display since Germany's effort in 1936. A countdown clock in the heart of Beijing ticked off the days as tens of thousands of migrant workers labored around the clock to complete the spectacular venues and spruce up the city. Nothing could be allowed to go wrong.

As the spring of 2008 gave way to summer, a malign demon seemed bent on wrecking the party. The Olympics were sold as environmentally friendly, but everywhere the symptoms of China's toxic industrial revolution were breaking through. International athletes threatened to boycott the games to avoid breathing Beijing's contaminated air. The city's officials quietly moved the air-quality monitoring stations to the suburbs in the hope of getting better readings. A toxic algae bloom of biblical proportions broke out in the coastal waters of Qingdao, threatening the sailing events. A full-scale revolt in Tibet and a catastrophic earthquake in Sichuan added to a litany of bad news that threatened to overwhelm even the Chinese state's capacity for propaganda. It was not a good moment to talk about dying babies.

The trouble for the babies had begun in June 2006. Spotting an opportunity in China's growing appetite for milk and dairy products, New Zealand's giant dairy enterprise, Fonterra, invested heavily in the Chinese market. Fonterra's biggest purchase was 43 percent of a Chinese dairy company called Sanlu, with whom they set up a joint venture that would ensure, the company boasted, a "world class dairy research and manufacturing capacity."

If the company's promises had been borne out, it would have marked a welcome improvement in a dairy industry that had already been responsible for some notorious scandals. In the worst one to date, in 2004, thirteen babies in Anhui Province had died as a result of consuming what turned out to be fake baby milk. No doubt in choosing Sanlu as a partner, the New Zealand enterprise was reassured by the fact that it was owned by the Hebei provincial government and, as China's leading infant-formula company, it had outsold its rivals for fourteen consecutive years. A month after the joint venture was set up, the Sanlu brand won an award. Sanlu's marketing promised that the group had "shouldered to the utmost degree its responsibility and mission to ensure the highest quality and safety of each bag of infant formula." The vice-CEO of the group, Wang Yuliang, promised perfect, high-tech production of its infant formula. After all, he said, "the quality of the product is the infant's life."

Doctors picked up the first signs of trouble in the spring of 2008: unusual clusters of infants were presenting with symptoms of kidney disorders. They duly reported their concerns to the Health Ministry, and a few journalists began to work on the story. By July 2008, a month before the Olympics, He Feng, a reporter on the well-respected newspaper *Southern Weekend*, knew of twenty babies in Hubei province hospitalized with kidney ailments. All had been fed Sanlu baby milk, which, unbeknownst to the babies' parents, had been contaminated with melamine.

Melamine is a chemical that can mimic protein and can be used to disguise the fact that milk has been watered down. It was the same substance that had killed a number of dogs in the United States in 2007 after they had consumed pet food in which melamine had been used to counterfeit rice protein and wheat gluten. The animals had died of kidney failure. The source had been traced back to China.

He Feng was not aware that he was looking at a case of widespread melamine adulteration, but he did know that something serious was going on with the nation's infants. His problem, though, was how to get his story published. In the countdown to the grand Olympics opening ceremony, China's propaganda bureau regarded bad news like this as close to treason. The censors repeatedly spiked his story.

Nor was there much enthusiasm in other parts of the Chinese state to investigate what might turn out to be a negative episode that could reflect badly on the national image. Sanlu had been certified as exempt from any supervision by China's overstretched health and food inspectors and the state inspectors, nominally the guardians of public safety, were clear that excessive zeal at such a delicate political moment would be unwise. The General Administration for Quality Inspection reported no problems with Sanlu's products; the Health Ministry's disease control center declined to respond to the growing number of reports from doctors across the country of kidney stones in infants; the Food and Drug Administration found nothing that merited intervention.

Sanlu and its majority shareholder, the Hebei provincial government, were aware of the medical reports but were equally clear that a food scare at such a moment would be commercially damaging. More important, any official who failed to do his national duty and suppress such negative news at such a sensitive moment could say good-bye to his career. Fonterra's baby milk stayed on the supermarket shelves. The stories were not published.

The Olympics were judged a success. The opening ceremony, choreographed by film director Zhang Yimou, was the most lavish in history, even if it was discovered later that some of its effects were digitally mocked up for TV. China had won a record haul of medals, and the tactic of deporting potential troublemakers from the capital, well out of sight of foreign journalists, had largely worked. By the time the Games were over, three hundred thousand babies had suffered kidney damage and eight had died.

Once the Olympic fever had died down, the dogged journalist He Feng returned to his story and located hundreds more cases in dozens of hospitals. But it was not until September 12 that, in a carefully calibrated loosening of the valve, the official Xinhua news agency finally reported that there was an anonymous accusation against Sanlu from Gansu Province. *Southern Weekend* was not allowed to publish its story for a further two days, until the contaminated baby milk was finally removed from supermarket shelves.

In the scramble to save careers and reputations that followed, the spotlight turned to the New Zealand investors and their role on the joint venture's main board. Fonterra's own account of its role in the scandal of the poisoned babies was that the company had struggled heroically to act with integrity despite obstruction from its Chinese partners and the Chinese authorities. Fonterra officials claimed that their first intimation of trouble came on August 1, six weeks before any public acknowledgment. They had remonstrated, they said, with their Chinese partners, and when Sanlu had refused to take the milk off the shelves, Fonterra had turned to the New Zealand prime minister, Helen Clark, for assistance. It was her intervention, they claimed, that finally worked, but only once the Olympics were safely over.

On September 15, two brothers who had supplied three tons of milk a day to Sanlu were arrested, along with seventeen others, including several Sanlu managers. The elder of the two brothers, a Sanlu supplier since 2004, admitted that he had been adding melamine to his milk for the best part of a year. Parents and doctors had begun to complain in March, and the press had been on the case by July. The Chinese authorities, however, claimed they had been unaware of the poisoning until September 8.

In the aftermath of the scandal, Sanlu went bankrupt and Fonterra wrote off $201 million in worthless shares. The milk producer and a supplier were executed; the former chair of Sanlu, a woman, was sentenced to life in prison; and sixteen others, mostly midlevel executives, were punished. The mayor and the party boss of Shijiazhuang, Sanlu's home base, were sacked. For the bureaucrats who had suppressed or ignored the scandal, there was no sanction. How could there be? They were obeying a central government order that nothing should be allowed to disturb China's big Olympic moment. The twenty-two other companies discovered to be selling melamine-tainted milk, a list that included one of the official suppliers to the Beijing Olympics, appeared to have escaped major punishment.

Nor was there any sign that the dead and sick babies had spurred the state to reform the morass of corruption and political interests that generated the affair. This was not the first milk scandal in China, but it was one of the worst. Hopes that the government might take steps to ensure it was the last proved illusory when, in February 2010, the authorities admitted that they had recovered more than 350,000 pounds of melamine-contaminated milk powder from across China. Some of it, they surmised, was stock salvaged from the product recall in 2008 and recycled back to the consumers.

By then, however, the state had found other miscreants to punish. In March 2010, in a court in Beijing, the trial opened of Zhao Lianhai, an advertising executive and father of a Sanlu baby. Zhao was a prominent campaigner for justice for the Sanlu victims and their parents. He had been demanding a level of compensation that would allow parents to pay for the continuing medical treatment their chronically sick children required. His actions had marked him out from the many parents who had been bribed or intimidated into silence. As his trial opened, Zhao had been languishing in detention for five months. Now he was facing charges of "chanting slogans and holding illegal gatherings" as well as "provoking many people to cause trouble," crimes against the harmony of the People's Republic that carry a five-year prison sentence. The trial closed again after a few hours. After keeping him a further eight months in detention, the court finally handed down its verdict. Mr. Zhao was sentenced to two years in prison for "inciting social disorder."

PART TWO

INSISTENT HOSTS

HOW HARRY LOST HIS EAR
~NORTHERN IRELAND~

SCOTT ANDERSON

"YOU'RE DOING WHAT?" MY GIRLFRIEND OF THE TIME ASKED.

I raised the beer bottle to my lips, took a good pull. "Training."

"Really? It looks to me like you're just drinking."

I finished off the bottle, moved it across the table to join the other empties, shook my head. "No. I'm drinking a lot faster than I normally do, and a lot more. That's why it's called training."

I didn't really expect her to understand; she wasn't a journalist.

Before embarking on a story, a journalist needs to prepare. That might mean reading background information, arranging interviews, whatever. If going to a war zone, it might also mean lining up a fixer, a translator, borrowing a buddy's flak jacket. To get ready for Belfast, which is where I was headed that summer of 1993, my preparations were a good deal simpler, if more physically taxing: to get my beer-drinking abilities up to a level where I could stay even with the Andytown Lads—which was another way of saying to a level that would cause the average person to curl up in a fetal position and wet himself.

I'd first gone to Belfast in 1985 with my brother for part of an oral history we were compiling on different conflict zones around the world. From the outset, there was something about the place that fascinated me. Undoubtedly part of it was that, being a culture very much like my own, Northern Ireland had none of the confusing exoticism of other war zones. Instead, it was like a little lab school for understanding how armed conflicts can start, how they can be perpetuated, the difficulty in ever bringing them to an end. Plus, it was a place where you had to work at getting hurt. Sure, as a visitor you stood the same random chance as the natives of being in the wrong place when a bomb went off, of being on the same sidewalk where gunmen were performing a drive-by shooting; but Belfast was never Baghdad or Beirut—hell, it was barely Detroit—and it wasn't like anyone was going to deliberately target an American journalist. It was a way to study the inner workings of war with very little risk.

After that first trip to Northern Ireland, I began going back for extended stays—a couple of months at a time, once for nearly four months—whenever my finances would allow. It wasn't altogether clear what I was doing there. I had vague plans to maybe write a book about it one day, perhaps just a long magazine feature piece, but my ongoing lack of productivity, the absence of anything appearing under my byline back in the States that might piss people off, had the pleasant effect of reassuring those who talked to me that I was harmless, innocuous.

One person who appreciated my continued journalistic inaction was a man I will call Seamus. He was in his mid-thirties, a former boxer with fists the size of bear claws, but now a small businessman with a young family. Despite his somewhat intimidating appearance, Seamus was actually a very sweet, funny guy, and we became fast friends, a friendship cemented over copious drinking sessions at out-of-the-way pubs in the Belfast city center. Eventually, Seamus introduced me to his closest mate, another former boxer whom I'll call Harry.

The two had very similar bios. They had grown up together in Andersonstown, a hard-line Catholic ghetto in West Belfast that was one of the principal strongholds of the Provisional Irish Republican Army, and both had signed on with the Provos when "The Troubles" started in 1969. In

1972, Seamus and Harry had been swept up in the British government's anti-paramilitary Internment campaign, and had spent the next four years in Long Kesh prison.

Physically, though, the two were very different. Seamus was a short, barrel-chested man with a quick smile and an easy laugh, quite handsome despite his broken nose and rough-hewn face. Harry was leaner, much taller, and wore a constant earnest frown that lent him a slightly befuddled manner, as if he were always straining to follow the conversation. But maybe having only one ear does that to a man, because Harry's most distinguishing feature was that the right side of his head appeared to have been melted away, just a mottled lump of scar tissue indicating where his right ear should have been.

Over time, our get-togethers expanded to include three or four other men, other friends of Seamus's from Andersonstown. Like him, they were in their mid to late thirties, and all had earned their Provisional stripes as younger men, either as foot soldiers on "active service" or by having been imprisoned during Internment. Now, by the late 1980s, their days of shooting and bombing were long behind them, and most had started families. They all described themselves as "businessmen"—even if, like Seamus, they never went into much detail about what that entailed.

As the group expanded, our gathering spots shifted from the bars in the "neutral" city center to the pubs and drinking clubs in IRA-controlled West Belfast, locations where the Andytown Lads felt more at ease. And as the numbers expanded, so did the amount of beer consumed.

There was a simple explanation for this. In Northern Ireland, drinking was done on the "round" system, which meant that when anyone went up to the bar for another beer, they bought for the entire table. It didn't matter if you had a full beer in front of you—or four or five full beers, as frequently happened to me in my novice days—you were about to get another one. There was also a rather unforgiving chivalric code that attached to the system: as a man, you couldn't beg off a round (pussy), or hand off your excess beers to a more accomplished companion (pussy), or drop down to half-pints (the mind shudders).

I was already well acquainted with the central role that beer played in Northern Ireland society. At the end of our monthlong stay in 1985, my brother and I had done a rough accounting of our expenses, and had figured out that just about 25 percent of all the money we'd spent—and bear in mind that this total included hotels, meals, rental cars, all the usual expenses of daily life—had been spent on beer. But that had been amateur hour. In hanging out with the Andytown Lads on my subsequent trips, the beer portion of my expenses easily approached 50 percent, maybe higher. These guys did not mess around, and it was only by learning the nuance of their language that I was gradually able to develop a kind of early warning system for the kind of night I was in for: getting together when the Lads were "on the wagon" meant having four or five pints, going out for "a drink" meant anywhere from six to ten, while "going drinking" pushed that number into the mid-teens at least, perhaps even into the low twenties.

Needless to say, this wasn't the sort of thing where you just showed up and hoped for the best. Through trial and error and a couple of humiliating outings early on, I learned to prep with a light meal of brown bread, cheddar cheese, and lots and lots of water; getting my bladder revved up beforehand appeared to trigger a flushing impulse, so that by late in the evening it was as if my body wasn't even absorbing the alcohol anymore, I was just pissing straight beer; or maybe I was just so drunk it seemed that way. And though it's somewhat counterintuitive, I also learned to avoid the lighter lagers—the Harps and so forth—because there was something about them that would leave me stupefyingly wasted before I'd even hit double digits. Much better was Guinness, the sheer heft of it seeming to take up some of the alcohol, rather like what happens when one drinks after eating a large meal—or a half-dozen large meals, as the case may be. My overriding aim on such occasions was to stay observant and reasonably coherent, to reside in that small space between knowing you really should go to the local hospital to get your stomach pumped, and still being able to formulate that thought in words.

If it was all a test of sorts, I apparently passed, because gradually the nature of our outings changed. Instead of meeting up on a weekend and whiling away the night at one dreary pub in West Belfast, the Andytown Lads took to suggesting midweek crawls when we'd all pile into a couple of cars and visit ten or twelve dreary pubs in a single night. A quick pint or two in one place, and then it was off to the next.

In my defense, it didn't actually take that long—maybe midway through the second crawl—for me to figure out what was going on. My newfound pals were running the protection rackets for the IRA. The rackets were one of the crucial cornerstones of the IRA's underground financial empire, and virtually all businesses in the neighborhoods they controlled paid into them. Presumably dunning the corner stores and candy shops was the province of enforcers lower down the chain of command—the Andytown Lads' portfolio seemed to consist exclusively of pubs and nightclubs—but it was the collective proceeds from the rackets, more than any other single revenue stream, that enabled the IRA to continue its "armed struggle."

Not that any of this was ever explicitly stated. Mere membership in the IRA drew an automatic four-year prison term, so none of the Andytown Lads ever volunteered their paramilitary status to me, nor did I ever ask. For the same reason, I would make a point of looking in another direction whenever one of the Lads, having briefly disappeared into a back room with a club owner or manager, would return carrying a bank satchel or small tote bag. Although I was dying of curiosity, even asking what had happened to Harry's ear seemed a topic too delicate to broach.

A line of sorts was crossed on the night Seamus took me to a club in South Belfast that I hadn't been in before. No sooner had we entered than the club owner, a twitchy middle-aged man named Kenny, hurried over to deliver an effusive greeting and usher us to a prime table overlooking the dance floor. As he watched Kenny scurry off, on his way to the bar to get us our drinks, Seamus gave a sly grin.

"I used to have problems with Kenny," he said, "because he just never saw the need for our security service. Then he got firebombed a couple of times. Now he loves to see me come around."

I became a regular tagalong on the Lads' "Tuesday night" runs (so called because the IRA's standard cut was roughly equivalent to the take on that slow—but not the slowest—night of the week). The owners and bartenders of these places got to recognize me. They were always very nice.

But what I also gradually came to understand was that, in providing the means for the conflict to continue, this underground economy had also transformed the conflict. It wasn't just the Provisionals. All the paramilitary organizations operating in Northern Ireland—the Provisionals' rivals on the Republican side, the various Protestant Loyalist paramilitaries on the other—now depended on the lifeblood of the protection rackets and their other criminal enterprises to survive. In the process, the war was no longer just a spiritual raison d'être for true believers on both sides, but an economic one, a source of livelihood for many, including my Andytown pals on their Tuesday-night runs.

Not that I was planning to get all high and mighty about any of it, but it was in hopes of further understanding this underworld aspect of the conflict that I made plans to return to Belfast in the summer of 1993. And in contrast to my past lassitude, this time I had two very specific objectives in mind. First, I was going to learn how Harry lost his ear. Second, I wanted to talk with someone high up in the IRA chain of command, someone who would be willing to discuss the inner financial workings of the organization.

But if I had any hope of achieving these goals, I had to be at the top of my game. At my girlfriend's house, I rose from the table, went into the kitchen, and brought out another six-pack.

"You're drinking *more?*" she asked.

"Training," I corrected. "Training more."

I'd been back in Belfast for nearly a month. I'd gone out on a couple of Tuesday-night runs, but this particular night was more on the mellow side of things, a gathering with the Lads at one of the IRA clubs just off the Falls Road. What with the wire-mesh grills over the windows, the anti–car bomb boulders out on the sidewalk, and the heavy security at the front door—no one got in here unless they were known—it was the sort of place where the guys felt most relaxed, were most likely to open up a bit.

Shortly after my return, I'd taken Seamus aside and told him of my desire to talk with a senior IRA commander. The request had discomfited him a little, but he said he'd see what he could do. I'd brought the matter up a couple of times since, not in any pushy way, and all I'd gotten from Seamus was that he was working on it.

In the meantime, it seemed a propitious moment to pursue my other objective on this trip, because by coincidence in the drinking club I was seated next to Harry. I leaned slightly in his direction.

"So tell me, Harry, what happened to your head?"

Harry turned to me with that befuddled look. "What's that?"

I saw my error. Dumb good luck had sat me next to Harry, but dumb bad luck had put me on his earless side. I had no choice but to raise my voice.

"What happened to your head?"

The others at the table all heard, of course, and for what seemed a very long moment, there was silence. Then the other Lads all started laughing uproariously.

I can't recall now how many of the salient details were provided by Harry himself and how many by the others, but the story's starting point was the day in 1970 when a teenage Harry had sought out his local IRA commander and asked to join up. As his initiation, Harry had been told to firebomb a particular Loyalist pub on the Shankill Road, a working-class neighborhood just three miles north of Andersonstown that was the heartland of the Protestant Loyalist enemy. The aim wasn't to kill anyone, just to gut the place, so Harry was told to hit the joint in the middle of the night.

He had absolutely no experience with arson, but from a couple of guys in the neighborhood Harry learned how to fashion a Molotov cocktail. He surreptitiously cased the Shankill Road pub. He decided the best approach would be to launch the firebomb through a second-floor window, since second-story fires tend to go undetected far longer than first-story ones and the place would be finished by the time the fire department got there. He carefully figured the height of the second-story windows, the arc and velocity he would need to get the Molotov cocktail up there.

Fashioning a homemade grenade launcher—really more of a slingshot—Harry spent a number of days perfecting his aim, figuring out exactly how much pull he needed to get the gasoline bomb through the window, precisely how many seconds he had after the fuse was lit before the bottle exploded. Finally satisfied, he set out late one night for the Shankill Road.

It being well past curfew, the Shankill was completely deserted, but Harry was still nervous as he set to his preparations. So nervous that he somehow failed to notice a crucial detail, that in response to the rash of firebombings that was gutting pubs all over Belfast, the Shankill Road joint had recently put mesh grills over all its windows.

Harry lit the fuse, he had his arc down perfectly, but to his considerable surprise he watched the bomb bounce off the enmeshed window, carom high up into the sky, and finally plummet down to explode right next to his head.

It took rather a long time for these last details to emerge, since the other Lads at the table were laughing so hard they could barely speak.

"There was talk around headquarters of trying to claim it was a Loyalist atrocity," Seamus offered, once the laughter around the table had subsided somewhat. "I mean, why else is a Catholic man running down the Shankill with his head on fire?"

This sparked a whole new round of giddy laughter, reinforced when one of the Lads decided to perform a dramatic reenactment of the incident, running around the table shrieking as he slapped at the imaginary flames engulfing his head.

At last, one of them tried to console the glowering Harry. "Aw, come on, it's a point of pride. You hear guys saying they'd give their right arm for the cause? Well, you gave your right ear."

About a half-hour later, the topic of conversation having long since moved on, a couple joined our table. The man, short and dark-featured with a bodybuilder's physique, appeared to be in his mid forties, while the woman was quite a bit younger—maybe late twenties—and attractive in a slightly trashy way; I'll call them Liam and Mairead. They were known to all the Lads, and pleasantries were exchanged, but the mood at the table noticeably changed with their arrival: a sudden vague awkwardness, a note of sobriety. Initially I attributed it to Mairead's presence—women were rarely a part of these gatherings—but when she went off to talk with a couple of girlfriends, the stiffness remained.

Liam sat across from me, and I noticed him occasionally glancing in my direction, as if trying to ascertain who I was. There seemed little in the way of genuine curiosity, however; whenever I made eye contact, his gaze was opaque, his face expressionless, impossible to read. I also noticed that he was exempt from the round system. He did have a beer in front of him, but it was largely ornamental, something he perfunctorily took small sips from.

After about twenty minutes he half-rose out of his chair, causing all conversation at the table to stop. "May I speak with you for a moment?" he asked me gently.

We went to a small table in a quiet, far corner of the club. Liam had very dark eyes, almost black, and they now had an intensity that hadn't been there before. "So, Seamus tells me you want to talk with an IRA commander," he said.

I nodded.

"You're talking to one." A brief pause. "I'm only doing this because you're a good friend of Seamus's, and I'll only answer your questions on the understanding that you never identify me in any way. If you ever violate that, it doesn't matter where you go, we will hunt you down and we will find you." Another pause. "Don't think of that as a threat. Think of it as a new fact in your life."

I nodded again, but inside I was thinking it was just about the coolest threat I'd ever received, wondering which movie he'd cribbed it from.

While it was quite early in the evening—which meant I still had my wits somewhat about me—I wasn't at all prepared to start an interview, and groped for the first question to ask. Liam raised a hand.

"Not here. We're going someplace."

A few minutes later, Liam collected Mairead and the three of us went out to the sidewalk, where a driver in a sedan was waiting. As we drove down the Falls Road, Mairead, totally incurious about why I was there, told a long and complicated story about the romantic travails of one of her girlfriends— something about another man, another woman, a bad case of shingles, and a vacation in Spain—to which I said nothing and Liam grunted at the proper intervals.

We turned in to a working-class neighborhood of old council houses, and the driver stopped before one in the middle of a nondescript block. It was identical to all the row houses on either side save for its bulletproof metal door and the four or five locks the driver had to manipulate to get us inside. It was the classic two-up, two-down row house that dominated West Belfast—I'd been in so many over the years that I could walk through them blindfolded—but the distinguishing feature of this one was the complete lack of any furnishings or knickknacks or personal touches that suggested someone actually lived there.

As Mairead puttered in the kitchen, Liam and I settled in the front room of the safe house. With rather remarkable forthrightness, he detailed the

Provisional's financial structure, the various enterprises—illegal or otherwise—that kept the guerrilla movement going.

"But yes," he said, "criminality is something we always need to be on guard against, but in this, there's a tremendous difference between us and all the other groups. You look at the Officials [the Official IRA], they're just a bunch of fucking gangsters. The same with the [Loyalist] UDA. With us, the vast majority of the money that's raised—I'd say 95 percent—goes straight into the armed struggle. With the UDA, it's what, maybe 5 percent? And that's why we're winning."

He had a point, because even its bitterest enemies conceded the Provisionals' reputation for discipline, for fiscal responsibility. But I was curious how that was maintained, why the lure of easy money didn't corrupt. Were the Provos really so ideologically pure?

"I don't think that's it." Liam smiled. "I think it's because when we find one of our people working a fiddle, skimming off the top, whatever, we kill them. We've got a proven track record on that."

We talked for a very long time. Of all the "hard men" I'd met in Northern Ireland, Liam seemed the hardest: measured, supremely self-controlled, a man driven by calculation rather than emotion. But then something altered that appraisal slightly, and it happened at precisely eleven o'clock.

Liam was discussing the IRA's "punishment squads," the young paramilitary wannabes who enforce discipline in the IRA neighborhoods, when his digital watch sounded the eleventh hour. He broke off in mid-sentence to go to the far side of the room and turn on a radio. The lead story on the BBC was of a British soldier killed that afternoon by a roadside bomb outside a small village in Derry province, the handiwork, it was presumed, of the IRA. As the report continued, Mairead came in from the kitchen where she had been relegated with a shocked look on her face.

"Liam, that's so weird," she exclaimed when the report ended. "I mean, we were in that village just yesterday!"

Liam fixed her with a baleful gaze, to which Mairead seemed utterly oblivious.

"I mean, it's scary, isn't it? I mean, it could have been us driving down that road when the bomb went off."

Every man has his Achilles' heel, and Liam's was named Mairead; if he ever got popped, I was quite sure it was going to be because of her.

By the time Liam and I finished talking it was hours past curfew, so I spent that night in the safe house, in a small spare bedroom at the top of the stairs. I was awoken in the morning by the sound of the television and a high, almost giddy laugh that I couldn't at all place. Coming down the stairs, I spotted Liam sprawled out on the carpeted living room floor watching a Road Runner cartoon, laughing like a child whenever the coyote got stomped or run over or blown up.

Late that afternoon, Seamus stopped by my hotel in downtown Belfast. I was surprised to see him because he'd never just dropped by unannounced before, and I knew he didn't really like coming into the neutral zone, felt much more comfortable up in the West Belfast "tribal areas." He seemed distracted, tried to chat about bullshit, but his heart wasn't really in it.

"So, how'd it go?" he asked finally.

"Good."

I could see he was relieved by this, as much by the brevity of my response as by its content; he didn't need or want to hear any details. He nodded, and then gazed down Shaftesbury Avenue—the so-called Golden Mile of Belfast, with its fancy shops and cafés and nice restaurants, an oasis of affluence that the authorities promised might be the future of all Belfast if only "The Troubles" could be brought to an end—and then turned back to me.

"So, you want to get a drink?"

WEIGHED DOWN BY
A GOOD MEAL
~GAZA AND ISRAEL~

JOSHUA HAMMER

I STOOD IN THE CORRIDOR OF A RAMSHACKLE BUILDING CALLED Beit Agron in central Jerusalem, the headquarters for foreign journalists and military and government spokesmen, shaking with rage and humiliation. Seconds earlier, I'd been called a liar and then physically ejected from the office of the Israeli government press director. Now, as I took a deep breath and headed down the stairs, I thought back to the incident that had led to this point—an innocent comment I'd made two years earlier about a meal, a compliment that would brand me in some people's eyes as a pro-Palestinian stooge—and wondered if that remark would ever stop haunting me.

It was May 29, 2001, when the phone rang over breakfast at my home in Jerusalem. My interpreter, Ali, was on the line, breathless with excitement, informing me that my weeks-long attempt to meet the leadership of the Popular Resistance Committee, a coalition of armed factions in Gaza, had come through. "You need to drive down immediately," he said. *Newsweek* photographer Gary Knight and I drove to the Erez Crossing, the checkpoint dividing Israel from the Gaza Strip, where we passed through a long corridor leading into Palestinian territory and caught a taxi to Gaza City. There we picked up Ali and sped along the coast, past fortified Israeli settlements and Israeli troops peering out through bulletproof slots in cylindrical guard towers, to a scruffy tea shop in the hardscrabble town of Rafah, on the border with Egypt, where we were supposed to meet our contact. He turned out to be an elderly man in shabby clothing and rubber sandals, who led us on foot through sand-filled alleys to a concrete-block house where five armed men in black ski masks were waiting for us.

The men searched us, then led us into a small and airless room. Our host, the commander of a cadre of Palestinian fighters who called themselves the Fatah Hawks, wore a black-and-white-checkered kaffiyeh wrapped tightly around his face, so that only his eyes were visible. Perched on a wooden chair and flanked by two bodyguards, he proceeded to deliver a monologue for half an hour about the armed resistance. For the most part, this consisted of boasts about the number of Israeli settlers and soldiers his men had shot and scathing criticism of the U.S. and British governments—"Bush and Blair"—for their support of Israel. The speech, delivered in Arabic in a low monotone, soon became repetitive; so when the commander, who went by the ubiquitous Middle Eastern nom de guerre Abu Mohammed, suggested a break for lunch, Knight and I could barely conceal our relief.

As if on cue, the door swung open, and two of Abu Mohammed's underlings—muscular men with black ski masks pulled over their faces and AK-47s slung over their shoulders—entered the room. They carried trays of hot and cold meze, an assortment of small dishes of traditional Arabic cuisine. The masked men set the trays on a low wooden table and beckoned Knight, me, and Ali to sit on pillows on the floor. "Please," urged our host, his voice muffled by the checkered cloth in front of his face. "Begin."

And we did. It was one of the most sumptuous spreads that I'd ever been offered during the six months I'd spent as *Newsweek*'s bureau chief in Jerusalem, shuttling between Gaza and the West Bank amid the intensifying violence of the al-Aqsa Intifada: Bowls of hummus gleaming with pools of olive oil and dollops of chickpeas artfully arranged on top. Baba ghanoush, a stew of eggplant and tomatoes spiced with garlic. A pot of dark, fermented fava beans, known as *ful,* that singed my tongue as I sampled it with a spoon. Fresh tomato and cucumber salad speckled with pine nuts; skewered chunks of chicken; succulent lamb kebabs; and piles of hot flat breads, straight out of the oven, charcoal-black and crisp in places, doughy and chewy in others. The gunmen-turned-waiters hovered around us solicitously, like some parody of the staff at the Four Seasons, wielding liter bottles of Coke, Sprite, and Fanta and refilling our glasses at every opportunity. Abu Mohammed joined us, tucking the lower part of his kaffiyeh underneath his chin so that his mouth would be freed up for eating. Knight and I dived into the spread ravenously, Then, when nothing remained but a few half-eaten pitas scattered among the empty plates, a large rectangle of baklava—gooey, oozing nuts and honey—made its appearance, served with glasses of tea and cups of Arabic coffee. When it was over, Knight and I reclined on our pillows, bellies bloated, awash in good feeling, marveling that in the middle of a war zone, the Fatah Hawks had played the role of hosts with such panache.

It was then that Abu Mohammed motioned for Ali to leave the room with him. Two minutes later, the interpreter slipped back inside. He looked stricken.

"Guys," he said. "There is a problem."

"What kind of problem?" I asked.

"It seems," he said, "that we have been kidnapped."

At the time of our abduction, the al-Aqsa Intifada was nine months old, and it was gaining force and fury across the occupied territories. Following the right-wing Israeli leader Ariel Sharon's provocative visit to the Temple Mount, or Haram al-Sharif, on September 29, 2000, angry Palestinians—already frustrated by the breakdown of the Camp David peace talks—had gathered at Israeli checkpoints, hurling stones and firebombs at soldiers. Israeli Prime Minister Ehud Barak ordered a swift and lethal response, and during the first two weeks of the uprising dozens of Palestinians, many of them teenagers, were killed by rubber bullets and live ammunition. Soon the armed wing of Yasser Arafat's Fatah movement, the al-Aqsa Martyrs' Brigades, muscled aside the stone throwers, firing on Israeli bases and ambushing settlers as they drove down bypass roads in the occupied territories. In late 2000 militants from the radical Islamic groups Hamas and Islamic Jihad, freed by Arafat from Palestinian Authority jails, regrouped and launched the first of what would become a wave of suicide bombings inside Israel. Sharon and his Likud Party were swept into power in February 2001 by an Israeli electorate disillusioned with Barak and attracted by Sharon's promise of a hard line against the uprising.

Nowhere did the violence seem more relentless, the confrontation more intractable than in Gaza, a sliver of overcrowded territory along the Mediterranean Sea, where roughly 1.2 million Palestinians shared the turf with 5,000 Israeli settlers. These Jews, who insisted that Gaza was their biblical inheritance, lived locked down inside fortresslike communities such as Kfar Darom and Gush Katif, protected by barbed wire fences and cordons of Israeli soldiers. To drive them out, the Popular Resistance Committee had embraced the tactics employed by Hizbullah guerrillas during the eighteen-year Israeli occupation of southern Lebanon: suicide bombings, roadside booby traps, ambushes, and mortar attacks. For the settlers, traveling beyond the perimeter of their compounds meant moving in armored convoys across miles of hostile territory, much as nineteenth-century wagon trains traversed the American frontier. The sandy wasteland was filled with buried roadside bombs; Palestinian snipers laid ambushes from half-finished buildings that offered a perfect vantage point over the highway. "The fighters aren't as sophisticated as Hizbullah, but they're getting better," Lieutenant Leor Bar-On, a Gaza-based Israeli soldier, told me during my reporting from the strip in May. "It's no longer a popular uprising. It's becoming a full-scale guerrilla war." Fueling the conflict was a constant flow of weapons passed to the militants through dozens of tunnels burrowed beneath the Egyptian border into Rafah, a highly effective smuggling operation dominated by a single Palestinian family.

In the polarized atmosphere of the al-Aqsa Intifada, meanwhile, the role of journalists covering the conflict had become excruciatingly difficult. More than any other place on earth, perhaps, reporters here were working in a fish bowl. The influential pro-Israeli lobby in the United States, as well as the Israeli right wing, parsed every word we wrote for traces of pro-Palestinian bias. They would fire letters to our editors and send volleys of e-mails if anything was perceived to have violated their notions of objectivity. When I wrote an article about Palestinians who lived in fear of being stoned by Israeli settlers on the road leading to their West Bank village, I received a torrent of correspondence accusing me of ignoring the sniper attacks on Israeli settlers by the al-Aqsa Martyrs' Brigades. (The accusation wasn't true; I'd addressed it in several previous articles.) The Palestinians, too, were highly sensitive to reporting that seemed to tilt too much in favor of Israel. But they lacked the sophistication, and the smoothly oiled media machine, to maintain the pressure that their Israeli counterparts were capable of. In our case, they opted for a cruder approach to make their point.

Now we sat on a couch in the airless room where we'd just eaten lunch, jolted by volleys of automatic weapons fire from just outside the window. Israeli bulldozers were knocking down houses along the border strip with Egypt, clearing an open field of fire, and the militants were shooting back. "Don't worry," Abu Mohammed said, in a feeble attempt at reassurance, "it's three or four houses away." The militants had confiscated our cell phones, and we were cut off from the outside world. Abu Mohammed handed Ali a typed press release in Arabic, apparently prepared by our abductors well ahead of time, that explained that we were being detained to protest U.S. and British government support for Israel. "We're going to be held until six o'clock," Ali said. "It's just a symbolic kidnapping." Assuaged by this promise, we sat quietly, dozing off in the hot afternoon, awakening occasionally to face the surreal sight of our armed guards staring at us through their black ski masks and kaffiyehs. But as the hours wore on we grew more nervous— especially after we learned that the terms had changed. Now, the commander told Ali, we would be held until "the Western media took notice." *What if nobody paid attention?* we wondered. *What if they put on a kidnapping and nobody heard?*

Knight and I tried to evaluate the situation calmly. True, Terry Anderson, the Associated Press bureau chief in Beirut, had been held for years by Hizbullah guerrillas, chained to radiators in a succession of tiny cells in the Lebanese capital's southern suburbs. But Gaza was smaller and still vastly more orderly than anarchic 1980s Lebanon, and the chances of our rotting here for the long term seemed highly unlikely. For that matter, Palestinian militants hadn't demonstrated a grudge toward Western journalists and indeed, usually seemed to cultivate us; they saved their antipathy for the Israelis. The Palestinian intifada would take a more virulent turn in the months ahead, with horrific suicide bombings in Israeli nightclubs and cafés and on buses (suicide attacks would escalate dramatically, from six in 2000 to eighty-four in 2001), and occasional threats against foreign journalists; in 2007 BBC correspondent Alan Johnson would be grabbed in Gaza by a militant group calling itself the Army of Islam, held for 114 days, and repeatedly threatened with execution. But this was all in the future. On top of everything else, that excellent meal seemed somehow reassuring. Would anyone who harbored evil intentions toward us have bothered to serve us such a spread? The gunmen were young, impetuous, immature, perhaps, but surely they didn't intend to harm us.

That assessment turned out to be correct. After three hours of isolation and mounting boredom, we were permitted to make cell phone calls to our head offices. I reached the editor-in-chief of *Newsweek,* Rick Smith, at eight o'clock in the morning New York time, and explained what was happening. One hour later, CNN broadcast the news of our kidnapping. Grinning behind his kaffiyeh, Abu Mohammed handed us our cell phones back and profusely apologized "for the inconvenience." The gunmen shook our hands. Abu Mohammed sent us on our way with an invitation to return the next day, "and we will serve you an even better lunch."

A taxi took us to the seaside apartment of Mohammed Dahlan, the Palestinian Authority's chief of preventative security in Gaza. Amid probing questions from the chain-smoking Dahlan, we dined on more meze and kebabs for two hours with what seemed like the entire upper echelon of the Palestinian Authority. No serious invitation in the Middle East, it seemed, could take place without piles of food and drink; it was a cultural code, a deep-seated sense of obligation, felt as intensely by the men who had kidnapped us as by the men who were now determined to hunt them down. According to Dahlan and his PA colleagues, the "Fatah Hawks" weren't members of Yasser Arafat's political organization at all, but rather "rogue elements" and "unruly youths" who needed to be punished. From the sharp tone of Dahlan's questions and the murmured asides to his generals and police commanders, I got the sense that there would be no second helping of chicken kebabs and flat breads with the Fatah Hawks. Our former captors, I presumed, were toast.

That night, on the drive back to Jerusalem, I gave a phone interview to a colleague at *Newsweek* in New York. Asked how we'd been treated during our four hours in detention, I told him that I'd only fleetingly felt in danger, and mentioned the feast that Knight and I had been served. Hours later, a short article appeared on the *Newsweek* Web site: "Hammer says he never feared his captors would hurt him or Knight. 'They never threatened us or pointed their guns at us,' Hammer says. 'They actually fed us one of the best meals I've eaten in Gaza.'"

I couldn't have imagined at the time that a single off-the-cuff comment about food, made partly in jest, would shadow me for the rest of my Middle Eastern tour. Yet within days the taunts, criticism, and, yes, outrage came pouring in. In the immediate aftermath, Israeli journalists phoned me simply to verify that I'd been quoted accurately. That should have been my tip-off. Soon, interviews conducted with Israeli politicians and military officers were invariably prefaced with, "Are you the guy who said his kidnappers fed him a good lunch?" Bestowing on me one of its Dishonest Reporting Awards for 2001, the pro-Israeli "media watchdog" site www.honestreporting.com declared, "One would expect a kidnap victim to be traumatized and angry. But Hammer had only compliments for his Palestinian captors, as described in *Newsweek*." A media critic named Samuel Bahn cited my comment as evidence of how Western journalists bent over backward to stay on good terms with the militants. "Journalists filing reports perceived to be harmful to the Palestinian cause, will not be likely permitted to reenter and could encounter a problem while in the territories," the blogger declared. "[After] *Newsweek's* Israel Bureau Chief Joshua Hammer was kidnapped . . . rather than criticize his kidnappers, Hammer had [nothing but] positive words for them." The *Jerusalem Post* made reference to the kidnapping in a discussion of an article I wrote in April 2002 about a teenage female suicide bomber and her teenage female victim. Despite my obvious pro-Palestinian sympathies as evidenced by the kidnapping experience, the writer declared, the piece about the bomber had shown surprising balance.

Even the *Princeton Alumni Weekly,* my college alumni magazine, referenced the kidnapping in a review of a book I later wrote about the intifada: "Hammer, who rejects charges of bias by some readers, sometimes has been a source of controversy himself. In 2001 a pro-Israel group criticized him for not voicing outrage over his own mini-kidnapping by armed Palestinians in Rafah to protest U.S. and British news coverage. After his release, Hammer said, 'They actually fed us one of the best meals I've eaten in Gaza.' He says he knew he wasn't in danger." By this point abductions of Western journalists and others by militants in the Middle East had become a serious, sometimes gruesome business. In 2002 terrorists affiliated with al-Qaeda had abducted *Wall Street Journal* reporter Daniel Pearl in Karachi,

Pakistan, and videotaped his decapitation. (The 9/11 mastermind Khalid Sheikh Mohammed would later claim that he personally executed Pearl.) And in chaotic Baghdad, al-Qaeda in Iraq militants had carried out a spate of kidnappings and executions of Western relief workers and contractors, including the Irish-born country director for CARE, Margaret Hassan. Amid the carnage and terror, my lighthearted comment praising militant hospitality seemed, perhaps, off-kilter. But it was made, I reminded myself, in a pre-9/11 world, a more innocent time. The divide had grown wider and the conflict uglier, and journalists, like relief workers and other noncombatants, had become fair game. The lavish meal seemed an expression of civility and hospitality that would be difficult to imagine now.

Then in early 2003, I visited the office of the Israeli media relations director in Jerusalem. A hawk-faced right-winger who routinely denied Palestinian translators accreditation and permission to enter Israel, the media man had taken a dislike to me shortly after my arrival in Jerusalem. The kidnapping and my praise of the militants' cuisine had intensified his antipathy. I'd gone to see him to follow up on a letter I'd written requesting permission to interview, for the book, an imprisoned suicide-bomb cell commander from the al-Aqsa Martyrs' Brigades. I had reason to believe that the media man either had never passed on the letter to the prison authorities, or had recommended that the authorities deny my request. I was pissed off and wanted an explanation.

He sneered at me when I confronted him in his office. "Eaten any good meals in captivity lately?" he taunted.

I told him I'd heard he'd intervened to stop me from interviewing the prisoner. "That's a lie," he said.

"I heard it from reliable sources," I said.

"You want to know something?" he said, coming out from behind his desk and moving toward me. "If it were up to me, I wouldn't let you inside that prison."

"What?"

"You heard me. I don't want to humanize these people. And that's exactly what you'd do."

"So you *did* block my request!"

"And everybody knows you staged your own kidnapping to get yourself some attention."

"Are you out of your fucking mind?"

And with that, he shoved me out of his office and slammed the door.

It has been nearly seven years now since anyone has confronted me with the incontrovertible proof of my pro-Palestinian bias—the meal comment. The last time was when I participated in a panel discussion at Princeton University during reunions in June 2004. I was there to discuss matters I thought were important—the future of peace in the Middle East, how to prevent yet more generations of Israelis and Palestinians distrusting and even hating each other—but a member of the panel came to the meeting with my lunch on his mind. "If you remember," he said, after I'd finished a spiel criticizing Israel's policy of targeted assassinations, which often ended up killing many civilians along with militants, "this is the journalist who praised his captors for the lunch they served him after taking him hostage in Gaza." My eyes rolled and I tried to answer him with a measured tone and more politeness than I had shown the Israeli press director.

In March 2011 I returned to Israel and the Palestinian territories, visiting the Temple Mount/Haram al-Sharif, historic Hebron, and other notorious clash points. The region was significantly calmer than the roiling mess I'd left behind in 2004, but it didn't take me very long to see how little, really, had changed. Once again I found myself whipsawed between Arabs and Jews, between settlers and (former) militants, between conflicting historical narratives. And once again I realized that in this charged environment, even the most innocent gestures can bring one grief. Desperate for a bite to eat outside the Tomb of the Patriarchs in Hebron—a holy site to which Muslims and Jews have shared access—I was faced with a choice: patronize the Jewish pizza shop favored by a settler acquaintance, or the falafel stand run by a friend of my Palestinian guide. I hesitated, I waffled, I looked them both in the eye. In the end, I decided to go hungry.

THE PRICE OF ORANGES

~PAKISTAN~

JASON BURKE

NOT MUCH HAPPENED IN ISLAMABAD IN 1998. NOT MUCH HAPPENED in Pakistan, in fact—or at least not much that troubled editors, viewers, readers, or policy makers in Europe or the United States. The country had slid inexorably away from international attention since the end of the war fought by the mujahideen against Soviet troops in neighboring Afghanistan almost a decade before. Most media organizations covered Pakistan from India. It was not a big story. The rediscovery of Pakistan and Afghanistan would come, with breathless haste, on September 12, 2001.

Just behind my apartment in Islamabad that year was a plot of land covered in mimosa trees, wild cannabis, and scrub. It was a graveyard, and though no one tended it or came to grieve at the dozen or so mounds of earth that lay among the rubbish under the trees, no one built on it either—though the potential for profitable development of such a prime piece of urban real estate was high. To one side of the graveyard was the substantial embassy of North Korea, to whom, it was whispered, Pakistan sold blueprints for nuclear bombs. These rumors were later proved to be at least partially true. Watching the embassy were two plainclothes intelligence agents, who usually sat on the pavement in the shade below a eucalyptus tree and read popular local-language newspapers. I knew them quite well after a while, and they smiled sheepishly when we greeted each other.

On the other side of the graveyard was the home of Benazir Bhutto. Those watching the Koreans could thus watch the former head of state, too. Out of power since her second government had been dismissed by the president on the prompting of the military two years before, Bhutto was fighting a series of graft allegations in the courts, and the intelligence services naturally wanted to know whom she was meeting. A few weeks after my arrival in Islamabad I was one of those giving their name to the bored policemen outside Zardari House—her home was then named after her controversial husband, Asif Ali Zardari, who had been in prison on corruption charges for several years.

I had received an invitation from Bhutto to come and "take tea." She was talking to her lawyers when I arrived, and for the first half-hour of our interview she went over what she claimed were the flaws in the case against her. She said she was a victim of a political conspiracy. This was at least partially true.

Since the death of military dictator Zia-ul-Haq in 1987, Pakistan had had four democratically elected governments. Two had been Bhutto's. Two had been those of her rival, Nawaz Sharif, scion of a Punjabi industrialist and leader of the Pakistan Muslim League. Sharif had been removed from power himself after a disastrous period from 1990 to 1993, but not before imprisoning Bhutto's husband. Back in power in 1996, Sharif had re-launched his investigations against his archrival. The allegations against Bhutto were serious, involving tens of millions of dollars in kickbacks, ownership of mansions in Britain, jewelry bought and held in Swiss banks. Bhutto's father, Zulfiqar Ali Bhutto, charismatic and cynical in equal measure, had founded his Pakistan People's Party, which his daughter had inherited, on a mix of populist socialist and nationalist rhetoric and with the slogan *roti, kapre, makan* (food, clothes, and shelter). If the PML was the party of the Punjab,

Pakistan's wealthiest province, and of rich businessmen or shopkeepers, then the PPP was supposed to be the party of the poor, especially the rural poor. The allegations of looting her country's exchequer, even if most were directed at her husband, hurt politically, if not personally.

Bhutto, forty-five years old, was wearing a blue *shalwar kameez* and her trademark white *dupatta* or scarf. Pearls the size of marbles dangled from gold clasps at her ears, and she wore a ring the size of a small matchbox on her finger on which I counted at least seventy-two individual diamonds in twelve rows. As she spoke she delicately nibbled cubes of *burfi,* sweetmeats popular throughout South Asia. *Burfi* is made from condensed milk cooked with sugar until it forms a solid cube of flaky paste. It is often mixed with rose water, cardamom, coconut, mango, pistachios, or cashew nuts, sometimes even cheese, all of which take the edge off the otherwise tongue-curling sweetness. Cut into mouthful-size blocks and saved for special occasions, *burfi* is decorated with flakes of silver foil and takes on a festive air.

It became very clear, very quickly, that Bhutto—despite the prospect of arrest and incarceration within days—was keener to gossip about the world at large than to talk about her own predicament. Conversation leaped from the almost surreally mundane to the enormously weighty with bewildering speed. One moment we were discussing the future of democracy in Pakistan or American policy in the Middle East, the next we were discussing new theories about the addictive properties of sugar or the latest trend in interior design or how her cat, Biscuit, had just had kittens. Bhutto wanted to know what I thought about the leopard skin that lay on the black tiles of her hall floor and the stuffed leopard that reared above it, and while we considered the golden stars painted on her ceiling she asked how long I thought Tony Blair was likely to remain in power in Britain.

We discussed books. Bhutto, whose taste for slushy romances was well known, said she had recently turned to "fun" biographies. Her favorite was a historical novel she had just finished about the life of Madame de Pompadour, the powerful mistress of Louis XV. And as tea stretched to dinner and we moved to the dining room, conversation broadened further. A servant brought out plates of barbecued chicken, kebabs, and stir-fried beef and bowls of dal (curried lentils), rice, and noodles. Bhutto picked at the heaped food in front of her, nervous, she admitted, of putting on weight.

She spoke about her time as a young woman at Oxford University, about the mass rallies that characterized her early political career in Pakistan as she campaigned for the restoration of democracy under the rule of Zia-ul-Haq, thereby fulfilling a promise made to her father in his prison cell hours before he had been hanged in 1979, the year the Soviets invaded Afghanistan. She spoke of the gifts she had been given during her two stints as prime minister. From Baroness Thatcher, whom she said she greatly admired and liked, she had received a blue-rimmed china soup bowl. Other world leaders had abandoned her after she had been forced out of power, but Thatcher had stayed in touch, she said. As far as Bhutto was concerned, the idea that Monica Lewinsky had seduced Bill Clinton was far-fetched. "He must have given her, you know, a look. . . . He's a Leo, you know, and so is my husband. Men like that . . . well. . . ." The sentence remained unfinished. She nibbled *burfi*, choosing carefully from a plate of the multicolored matchbox-size sweets, long fingers hesitating between those with almonds embedded in them and those with pistachios.

As I was leaving she asked me if I would like to go down to Naudero, her country home six hundred miles to the south and the seat of the Bhutto dynasty, for the commemoration of her father's "martyrdom." She had just had a new guesthouse completed, her children would be there, and it would be "just wonderful" if I could make it. In the garden of her home, her staff were singing prayers, interwoven with chants in the Sufi Muslim tradition, a call for God's help for the coming court appearances and for the trials and tribulations to come.

As the sun went down, the bright colors of the trees and the dust and the wheat became flat. Everything turned to tan and gray and rust. The small low villages, often just an uneven group of mud-walled houses clustered below a few palms, became difficult to pick out against the pale earth around them. Everywhere there were reservoirs and canals and streams. Buffaloes stood up to their necks in the water below thick clouds of mosquitoes, eyes white in the gathering darkness. On fallow fields there were small groups of herdsmen and Gypsy families camped behind piled bracken fences, cooking in small battered metal pots over furze fires, their livestock tethered nearby.

It was evening and my first sight of the interior of Sind. The province had been a desert until the British built a vast system of irrigation canals in the early part of the twentieth century. The surface of the land is now divided into small plots of crops—mainly rice, some wheat. There is a lot of fallow or waste ground—often a result of the irrigation raising the water table. As the water evaporates through the soil, it leaves mineral deposits behind. The soil becomes too salty to cultivate and reverts to dust and scrub. As a result the patchwork of fields is uneven, broken by long stretches of salt. As dusk came, the salt patches reflected what was left of the light. We passed a herd of camels trudging sedately along the side of the road. We drove on.

Eventually we arrived at a small rural town, fluorescent lights swinging above the tea shops and cheap restaurants bright and green after the darkness of the desert around. This was Naudero, the Bhutto family seat.

Centuries of Western visitors have written of the fabulous hospitality of their Asiatic hosts. Two elements are often missing from their accounts. The first is that feeding followers and visitors was for centuries an essential element of the redistribution of resources on which the quasi-feudal system existing across much of South Asia or the Middle East depended. The second is that hospitality is also an excellent means of control. Guests eat and sleep where they are told. Equally, those they meet can be carefully selected, what they see is restricted. In the most delicate and delightful of fashions, the guest is placed under the authority of the host.

To celebrate the anniversary of her father's death, Bhutto had gathered her faithful retainers. Sitting at the head of the dining room table in

Naudero like a sixteenth-century English monarch surrounded by her lords temporal and spiritual, she listened attentively as the senior barons of her party described the political situation in their domains. They sat in order of seniority. Opposite her, at the far end of the table, was Shabbir Ahmed Khan Chandio, the second most senior man of a tribe, numbering over a million people, almost all of whom would vote as he told them to. His family owned land the size of an average-size American state along the border with the vast neighboring province of Baluchistan. To his right was Makhtoum Shahabud-din Makhtoum, who had been finance minister in Bhutto's second adminis-tration. His land was so extensive that he claimed genuinely to be unaware of its exact size. Like Bhutto, he was also to be worshipped by several hundred thousand people as a spiritual leader, a saint, a *pir*. When Makhtoum spoke about "my villages" or "my people," the use of the possessive pronoun was entirely appropriate.

The dining room was the inner sanctum. Outside the house was a paved courtyard and a small zoo with antelope, deer, and a giant turkey. Beside the small, wonderfully carved, natural wood door to the main house was a large shaded area decorated with giant paintings of Bhutto and her father. This veranda was covered with plastic chairs and acted as Bhutto's waiting room.

When she was in Naudero Bhutto held audiences for her followers. They lasted entire afternoons. Outside her front door several hundred locals— mainly men but some women—milled around the courtyard hoping to be summoned to see her. The women wore burkas, the all-covering cloak with a mesh aperture to see through made famous by the Taliban in Afghani-stan but worn across much of the region long before the hard-line Islamic movement came to power in Kabul in 1996. Every so often a dozen or so supplicants would be shown in to the front room of the house, and Bhutto would listen to their problems and promise solutions. To one side, a servant kept a tray with a plate of Quality Street British supermarket chocolates and a box of *burfi* on it. Every ten minutes or so, Bhutto would take one, hesitating as ever as she chose. As the afternoon wore on, the rate at which the tray was brought to the small dais on which Bhutto sat accelerated.

The weekend climaxed in the rally to commemorate the death of Bhutto's father. For days local PPP organizers had been working to gather a big crowd. The buses and trucks had been trawling the surrounding villagers picking up Bhutto supporters and paying others and bringing all of them to the huge shrine that their leader was building as a dynastic tomb close to Larkana. It was unfinished—work having stopped when she was last ejected from government—but it was vast.

A podium had been set up a few hundred yards from the shrine and on it, in front of a crowd of ten or fifteen thousand, was gathered almost the entire political leadership of the PPP. In their starched white *shalwars* and designer shades it was difficult to imagine that they had anything in common with the masses sweltering in the sun in front of them.

Bhutto was, as is customary in South Asia, an hour or two late. Her speech was unexceptional, a lengthy shrill diatribe against the government and an effusive eulogy to her father. The crowd was large but not very large, and she failed to excite them very much. Her mind appeared to be on other things.

A few weeks later three judges, including the son of one of those who had sentenced her father to death, found her guilty of accepting bribes. Bhutto called on her supporters to fight the "fascist regime." Only in Naudero was there any response. Elsewhere there were a few sit-down protests and the odd demonstration. But there were no mass gatherings, no outbreaks of mass violence, no nationwide campaigns of civil disobedience. Bhutto slipped quietly out of the country and into exile.

Bhutto's exile was to last eight years. It is ironic in retrospect that she was thus to watch the return of her homeland to a major role on the international stage from the stalls. The attacks of 9/11 should have helped Bhutto in many ways. She was after all the archetype of a sort of moderate Muslim leader—Oxford-educated, a woman, adept at convincing and charming

Western interlocutors (especially men). Yet in President Pervez Musharraf, the army chief who had taken power in 1999 in a bloodless and relatively popular coup, she came up against a new and favored American ally and apparent friend of President George Bush. Bhutto, despite a formidable, well-funded, and effective lobbying effort in Washington, D.C., and elsewhere, found herself marginalized. She was unable either to return to Pakistan, where new laws banned her from prime ministerial office, or to establish an international role. She spent much of her time in Dubai, where her children were at school, and visited London regularly. Every time we spoke her frustration, though carefully concealed, was evident. Many politicians have returned from periods of internal or external exile stronger and more effective than when they left. Not Bhutto, however. Pakistan changed radically in the eight years that she was away, and not in ways that made any eventual return easier.

Five main trends were working against Bhutto. The first was that, given a choice between apparent stability under Musharraf, who also projected a moderate, pro-Western image and was good at charming his interlocutors, and Bhutto, the choice for America was clear. Yes, she was moderate, relatively secular, and pro-Western. But she was also willful, unpredictable, and very unpopular with Pakistan's security establishment. Until Musharraf began to be seen as more of a liability than an asset, from about 2007, no one was prepared to take the risk of backing Bhutto.

Second, there were genuine doubts over Bhutto's ability to control the rising tide of militancy in Pakistan if she did make a return to power. Although the real deterioration came after 2006, within even a year of 9/11, violence was soaring. As a frequent visitor to Pakistan throughout this period, I watched the growing toll of the bombings and shootings with pain and concern. The ground I could safely cover within the country became more and more restricted. Everything that had made Pakistan not just passionately interesting intellectually but a genuinely enjoyable place to be disappeared. There were many people whom I could no longer visit. The fabulous, often savagely beautiful landscapes that I had driven, ridden, trekked, even skied through would now have to wait for a better, happier time. One gastronomic pleasure after another dropped away, too. One of the constant delights of Pakistan had been the food. Once I had sampled astonishing chicken cooked with oranges at a graduation ceremony at a madrassa (religious school) deep in tribal territory close to the Afghan border. Such a meal was soon unthinkable. By 2008 grilled trout fished from mountain streams in the Swat Valley, 150 miles from Islamabad, was off the menu too, with fishing in remote areas rash to say the least and Swat itself partially under the control of newly formed Pakistani Taliban groups. Soon even eating out in the frontier city of Peshawar, where once I had shared mixed mutton curries cooked in iron pans over coals with local journalists in the main bazaar, was too risky. So too were the platters of Kabul-style pilau rice with meat, raisins, and carrots in the vast smugglers market on the road to the famous Khyber Pass. The aftermath of 9/11 in the restive zones along the frontier had seen a globalized radical Islamic identity fuse with a local tribal and ethnic particularism to form a potent and combustible combination. Bhutto did not seem to be the best candidate to counter it.

A further factor militating against Bhutto was a new political consciousness among Pakistanis. As with the extremism described above it would be wrong to overstate this—a huge proportion of Pakistan's 170 million inhabitants neither subscribed to a "jihadist" vision of Islam nor could be described as politically conscious in a Western sense either—but a significant change had nonetheless taken place. Partly because of the penetration of satellite television into every village and many homes in the country and the vociferous and lively (and often ill-informed and inaccurate) political debates that were their most popular programs, the old hierarchies were being questioned. Landowners who had once taken their authority for granted were finding that authority being questioned in an unprecedented way. If political process in Pakistan was moribund, political debate, albeit of an often depressingly low standard, was very much alive. New actors were emerging, such as the lawyers who were to play a key role in the eventual defeat of Musharraf, and new civil society groups. The political environment of Pakistan was evolving, changing, becoming more complex as every year passed.

Two other key processes were under way of which Bhutto appeared, in our many conversations in this period, largely unaware. The first was the enrichment of a substantial segment of Pakistani society in the miniboom sparked by Musharraf's economically liberal policies, easy credit, the lifting of sanctions post-9/11, the influx of remittance money as Pakistanis began to feel less secure in the West or the Middle East, and the new aid that began arriving. At the same time, Pakistan's cities and towns continued to suck in millions of people from rural areas. The result of these two processes was the creation of a new urban lower middle class. You only needed to stand on the corner of a Karachi street for a minute to see this. The families who had owned only a motorbike now owned the tiny 800 cc Suzuki Mehran car. Those who had had a Mehran now had a Corolla. Equally important were the values of this growing swath of the population. The late 1990s and the post-9/11 era had seen a hardening of Islamic identities at the expense of more pro-Western identities across the Muslim world. Pakistan was no exception. The new lower middle classes, millions strong, saw links to the West as suspicious, a marker of foreign dominance. The aspirational example had become the Persian Gulf. The dream holiday was no longer Europe or the United States, for which visas were difficult and the atmosphere for visiting Muslims unpleasant, but the United Arab Emirates or Malaysia. For such people, raised on a diet of news and discussion heavily informed by the prejudices once restricted to hard-line Islamists, the world was run by imperialist Americans and their Jewish allies who hated Muslims, the Taliban were righteous mujahideen, and the Indian secret services, or Mossad or the CIA, were behind most of the ills of their country. They were culturally, socially, and religiously conservative nationalists. They were increasingly numerous, increasingly dominant in public conversation, increasingly dominant in the security establishment. They were not, it is fair to say, natural voters for Bhutto, but nonetheless Bhutto gave no sign of having recognized this new tendency. When she spoke of Pakistan she spoke of "my nation," "my homeland," even "my people." But the Pakistan she wanted to come back to—to reclaim—was not the Pakistan she had left.

Zardari House had become Bilawal House, named after Bhutto's young son rather than her controversial husband. The lane that led to it was clogged with the concrete blast walls that, after a decade of covering the various theaters of conflict in the War on Terror, were wearily familiar to me. I negotiated three checkpoints and was shown into a small lounge. On the table were a flask of rose water and a small plastic tray of *burfi*.

It was December 2007 and Bhutto had been back in Pakistan for less than three months. Her return was largely the result of President Musharraf's internal and external weakness. Inside Pakistan, the former general's erstwhile popularity was long gone and his authority had been undermined by angry lawyers, an increasingly confident opposition, an economic downturn, and the security situation. Musharraf's primary justification for holding on to power was that he brought stability. But a series of bloody suicide bombings had made very clear the extent to which his rule had seen local militant groups establish themselves as a genuine threat to Pakistan as well as to the region. The growing evidence of the Pakistani security establishment's continued support for elements within the Afghan Taliban, whose senior leadership remained based in Pakistan, and their apparent reluctance to move seriously against the panoply of extremist groups operating on Pakistani soil, had sapped support for Musharraf overseas too, particularly given the vast military aid that had been supplied to the Pakistani army. The ideal, it was decided in Western governments, would be for Musharraf to remain president and for Bhutto to become prime minister.

Partly through the work of British diplomats, a deal was worked out in the summer of 2007 and Musharraf agreed to Bhutto's return, as well as that of Nawaz Sharif, her political archrival. Before she left Dubai, she told me that her slogan in the campaign for the parliamentary elections due in January would be *roti, kapre, makan*—that of her father in the 1970s. The corruption allegations were long forgotten. Bhutto landed in Karachi in October, to be greeted by a massive bomb that killed eighty in the procession leading her from the airport to the tomb of Mohammed Ali Jinnah, the Quaid-e-Azam, the great leader and founder of Pakistan.

By early December she was in full campaign mode. Every day she left Islamabad, driving long distances to rallies in the Punjab, Pakistan's easternmost province. This was not where Bhutto was most popular, and it was far from the family's hereditary heartland of Naudero and northern Sind. She also headed west, toward the Afghan border, into the North-West Frontier Province. Politically this made some sense. In this area, ruled for several years by a coalition of religious parties, popular opinion was running against the radicals, who had notably failed to improve roads, schools, health care, or any of the bread-and-butter issues that so often determine voting. Personally, however, Bhutto was taking a very significant risk. She had already survived one assassination attempt and had publicly stated that many wanted her dead—although those she named were probably not those responsible for the bombing in Karachi. Nor was winning votes in gritty towns like Charsadda or Nowshera vitally important to any electoral strategy. But Pakistan was "her homeland," and to reclaim it she needed to feel that no place was forbidden to her.

We left about ten o'clock, driving very fast on the new motorway that links Islamabad to Peshawar and cuts the journey time from four to two and a half hours—or less if you are traveling in a motorcade of a dozen vehicles with armed escorts. By noon we had reached Nowshera, a large town and army garrison thirty miles short of Peshawar and fifty-five miles from the Afghan border and one of the places frequently targeted by the militants. Once Afghan refugee camps had lined the roads around the city. They had gone, but the madrassas had not. They are not the suicide bomber factories they are often said to be, but are part of a broad transnational network linked to the rigorous and literalist Deobandi local southwestern strand of Islamic observance increasingly dominant in western Pakistan, particularly among the Pashtun tribes. Bhutto, a Shia steeped in Sufi traditions—westernized, moderate, secular—was everything they detested.

Bhutto lunched with local activists and members of Parliament, and the rally began. The local candidate in the forthcoming elections made a sycophantic speech. The crowd, sitting in long lines on the ground and carefully segregated, cheered and Bhutto took the stage. There are people who want to rob Pakistan of its future, but we will not let it happen, she told them. "There are those who abuse Islam for their own political ends and turn Muslim brother against Muslim brother." They cheered. "My government will bring you what you need: roads, water, electricity, *roti, kapre, makan*." More cheers.

And then it was over and she was gone and calling me over. Still breathless after forcing our way through the crowds, we climbed together into her heavily armored four-wheel drive and, amid sirens and horns, pushed out onto the main road that led to the motorway. We had gone only one hundred yards before she called for the hatch in the roof to be opened and stood up, waving to the traffic and to those along the roadside, receiving bemused acknowledgment in return from people who only after she had passed recognized who had just bestowed a regal wave upon them.

Stopping the convoy beside the market, Bhutto got out of her vehicle and, flipping her white *dupatta* over her hair, headed off among the stalls, asking the price of fruit. In her wake, overweight policemen tried to control the crowd, with little success. We were in Pabbi, a scruffy road-stop town that had been the site of one of the biggest militant training camps in the early 1990s. Working her way back to the vehicles, she brandished a bag of oranges like a lantern before her. "I wanted to know the price, Mr. Burke," she said, exhilarated by her own daring in making the unscheduled stop. "I need to get back in touch with Pakistan. The price of oranges is important. . . . And you stay safe by being unpredictable."

I interviewed her formally for an hour in the car as we drove back down to Islamabad on the road she proudly, and without foundation, claimed the credit for building.

I reminded her that a decade before at Naudero I had told her, to the shock and concern of her courtiers, that I thought she would be out of power for at least a decade. Bhutto laughed and asked me what my next prediction would be. She told me she had never expected to be out of power so long. "Are you on the brink of power now?" I asked.

"I think the people are with us and we have the momentum," she said. "And the international community is supporting a return to democracy."

Her biggest concerns were security and vote rigging at the polls in January. She was convinced the elections would be manipulated, the only question was how badly. "It's all in the numbers," she said. She also spoke of how she did not want Pakistan to be a base for international militancy—partly because the West was suffering from international terrorism but more because it was her own nation that was hurting most. She would be making more impulsive visits to markets, she said, because she needed to "meet the people."

Then, once I put my notebook away, she relaxed, slipping off her flat shoes, calling to her personal secretary in the front seat for sweets and sandwiches. Two Tupperware containers were passed back, one full of neat cubes of *burfi*. She spoke about those she said were trying to kill her—a cabal of retired senior military officers and intelligence agents in league with radical Islamic militants "embedded in the country" who formed a secret parallel state of immense power, she said. She spoke, too, about the long summer negotiations with Musharraf.

"What do you call him when you speak on the phone?" I asked.

"General Sahib," she said, smiling.

And what does he call you?

"Bibi," she said.

It was long dark by the time the motorcade halted outside Bilawal House. We said good-bye. She invited me once more to tea and to Naudero. "It will be just like old times," she said. Ten days later she was killed at a rally in the city of Rawalpindi about ten miles away.

Coconut *Burfi*

2 cups sugar
1 cup water
2 cups shredded coconut
1 ounce cashew nuts, coarsely ground or crushed
1 teaspoon ghee
1 teaspoon ground cardamom

Boil the sugar and the water together in a pan for 15 minutes to create a syrup and then add the coconut. Boil the mixture for another 15 or 20 minutes, stirring all the time.

At the same time, toast the cashew nuts in the ghee.

When the coconut syrup is thick, add the cardamom and cashew nut pieces and stir. Pour onto a greased plate and, using a knife, score the flattened mixture to create diamond-shaped pieces.

When it's cold you can cut it up and serve.

JEWELED RICE

~IRAN~

FARNAZ FASSIHI

ON A HOT AFTERNOON IN THE SUMMER OF 2003, I WATCHED THE abduction, at gunpoint, of three student activists belonging to a prodemocracy movement in Tehran. They were standing only a few feet away from me. The gunmen appeared, seemingly out of nowhere, as I discussed where to eat lunch with a few of my journalist friends.

We were leaving a press conference organized by Iran's main student movement, the Office for Fostering Student Unity. The press conference had dragged on and turned out to be a nonevent. The students had announced that they were in fact canceling a large demonstration planned against the government.

We huddled in a small room in the middle of the dry heat of a particularly baking July day without air-conditioning. A single fan whirled the hot air around the room. Sweat dripped down my neck, my hair sticky and wet under a blue silk scarf. I dutifully scribbled down a few quotes, and soon the thoughts of lunch began.

I craved delicious Persian food, the kind that my grandmother would take hours to prepare and then serve with pride. Fluffy saffron rice layered with sour cherries and slivers of pistachio and almonds, called jeweled rice, or a thick simmering stew of tiny eggplants and tomatoes flavored with dried lemons and a spice mix of cinnamon and cardamom.

Where would be the closest restaurant that served the most decent food downtown? Anyone who has ever traveled to Iran can attest that Persian cuisine is one of the richest and most varied in the Middle East. But much like the lives of the country's citizens, the food suffers from a dual identity: there is the private food, sensual and delicious, found only behind closed doors at home; and there is the public food, bland and standardized, served at restaurants around town.

Why? Iranians like to eat out—the restaurant business remains one of the most lucrative—but they want different food from what they find in their own kitchens. Eating out is also pricey and considered entertainment for families, who usually opt for pizza, sandwiches, hamburgers, or grilled kebab meats.

On one of my earlier reporting trips to Iran, the same abducted student activists who hosted the press conference had introduced me to their new favorite restaurant, called the Artist House Café. Perhaps we could all grab lunch there after the press conference, I thought, because it served home-made dishes with a twist and the students would feel at ease at their favorite spot to talk candidly about the brewing dissent among reformers.

The Artist House Café is unusual in many ways—it is the hangout place for student activists but also for intellectuals and artist types, located in an old brick building that was once part of a military base in the center of town. The building also sits in the middle of a beautiful garden with tall cypress trees, rose bushes, and small blue pools.

Modern statues made of bronze and stone are interspersed among the trees and flower bushes. A cozy art gallery in the corner displays the latest artwork of the budding artist community that has emerged under the rules of the Islamic Republic, which mandate that artistic expression fit religious sensibilities. Nude and sensual images are forbidden in paintings, so artists have become creative in expressing their true intent while superficially abiding by the rules.

The Islamic Republic's strict social rules mandate that young men and women not socialize publicly, and schools and even some university classes are segregated. However, youth have consistently bent the rules by finding friendly places, such as the Artist House Café, in which they can mingle. Tehran's mountain trails, parks, and cinemas are other popular destinations for young people. The first time I ate at the café in 2002, student members of the Office for Fostering Unity had invited me to attend one of their weekly meetings over dinner. In Iranian culture, the exchange of information—from family gossip to political secrets—centers primarily on a meal.

I happily gorged on the creative, strictly vegetarian menu prepared from classic Persian recipes. The food was a kind of experiment in fusion Persian; each little dish was its own political statement, the culinary expression of the shifting mood of the young people. The tofu replacing lamb chunks in the classic favorite *ghormeh sabzi* stew seemed like more than just a postmodern interpretation of Iranian cuisine. In that atmosphere, it also reflected the yearning for change in Iran's society—not the kind of change that forsakes tradition, upends cultural norms, and throws out your grandmother's best recipe for fried chicken, but a slow-cooking, reformist version of Iran in which, ideally, religion and tradition could complement democracy, not stifle it. The students, a group of a dozen young men and women, sipped fresh pomegranate juice and planned for a campus sit-in to protest the death sentence handed down to a professor who had said that people should not "follow religious teachings blindly like a monkey."

A young woman named Setareh read out bullet points of a speech she was preparing for the sit-in. She touched on the importance of free speech in an academic environment and how a new wave of student arrests had sown fear and panic on campus. Another student, Sajad, suggested that they also enlist a few reformist-minded professors to back them up with their own speeches.

I listened with fascination and envy. I had also attended college in Iran, at the very same university as some of these students, in the early 1990s.

But our college years were completely devoid of political activism. In fact, a kind of apathy ruled back when I was a student. Unlike the students sitting before me, with their lofty ideals of reform and practical ideas about how to execute them, my generation believed we were powerless to change the status quo. The reform movement, which took Iran by storm in 1997 with the election of President Mohamad Khatami, had not been born then.

During my college years, mornings and afternoons were withered away sipping cappuccino and café glacé at the then-popular Café Theater. We didn't even bother reading the newspaper, because back then our choice was between two government-owned papers, one more dreary than the other. We discussed love affairs, parties, and also literature and art. But mostly my friends and I plotted our escape from Iran. Mine would be easy, a return to the United States, where I was born and had lived for a decade after the revolution.

Our food options in the early 1990s were no more exciting than our newspapers. Our beloved Café Theater did not serve food. It was strictly a coffee joint, but thanks to the growing patronage of lingering hungry students, the owner—a shabby, chain-smoking, long-haired artist we called Uncle—finally put one item on the menu: an unimaginative cheeseburger and fries, served with a side of Iranian-made ketchup and mayonnaise.

It wasn't uncommon for Uncle to walk over to a table of young men and women, especially nonregulars, and segregate them by sending the girls upstairs. Or he would ask women to put their cigarettes down. He feared the morality police, who sometimes made the rounds in popular cafés and threatened to fine the owners or close their shops.

At the Artist House Café, however, change was everywhere. A stack of more than a dozen daily newspapers carrying a colorful array of political views, from ultraconservative to reformist, was available to read. Young men and women mingled freely for hours and often tables merged, forming one big party.

The vegetarian menu changed daily, based on the season and market availability. The restaurant was Iran's answer to Chez Panisse. The manager was a cheerful Iranian yogi who kept a basket near the café's entrance with leaflets advertising spiritual lessons, meditation, and yoga classes.

He served an exquisite sampling of six courses in small glass bowls placed tastefully on a large round copper tray for each individual. A typical meal included a lentil soup; diced salad of cucumber, tomatoes, and mint; a mini bite-size eggplant-cheese pizza; saffron rice with lentils and caramelized raisins; a tofu stew cooked with chopped fresh herbs such as cilantro and chives. Dessert might be custard with Persian mulberries. No alcohol is served in public in Iran, so to drink you would get a healthy glass of fresh watermelon or pomegranate juice decorated with a bright paper umbrella.

I had precisely this platter in mind that July day when I spotted the first gunman. He looked almost obese, his fat tummy bulging against the buttons of his checkered shirt, which was untucked over his baggy gray pants. His movements were swift, as if he was in a hurry, and his eyes darted around. I noticed him because he looked out of place.

He grabbed one of the students by throwing an arm around the student's neck. With his other hand, he pointed a gun at the student's head.

The student's black leather pouch dropped to the ground with a thump. His scrawny body wiggled, his legs jerked, his arms flapped. The man tightened his grip on the student's throat to still him. The student's cheeks flushed. He gasped for air and gagged.

We were standing on the sidewalk of Mottahari Avenue, one of central Tehran's busiest intersections. Shops were open all around us. Traffic whizzed by. Passersby crossed the streets.

When the student finally let out a scream, I also screamed.

"Shut up, shut up. Do you hear me?" the man yelled at me, briefly removing his gun from the student's forehead to point it toward where I was standing with my journalist friends.

Two other gunmen emerged from a car dealership next door. They abducted two other students in the same fashion as the first one, with guns pointed at their foreheads. The students were dragged and shoved inside two unmarked cars parked at the curb. One of the gunmen kept glancing back at us, waving his gun in the air.

Although they wore plainclothes, it was easy to identify them as members of the Basij paramilitary force. They had that stony expression of hate and rage in their eyes. I had seen that look many times before when Basij members waved their daggers, batons, and chains to disperse crowds of anti-government protesters.

The Basij are a voluntary task force, estimated to be between one million and three million, who act as the Islamic regime's chief enforcers. The Basij's official—they are under the command of the Revolutionary Guards—and yet unofficial, nonuniform status allows officials to play a charade of accountability. The government claims ownership of the Basij when it wants to show high numbers of supporters on election days and at government-sanctioned demonstrations, but then it disowns them if their brutal actions come back to haunt or embarrass the regime in any way.

In July 2003 the United States had just invaded Iraq. In less than two years, the United States had successfully removed two of Iran's top enemies, Saddam Hussein in Iraq and the Taliban in Afghanistan. But the Islamic Republic was now sandwiched, from east and west, between borders that housed massive American military bases.

At home, reformists were deadlocked in a political battle with conservatives. After years of unsuccessfully trying to reform the Islamic regime, reformers, long viewed as part of the establishment rather than as challengers, were morphing into a serious force of internal opposition.

The regime felt understandably nervous and vulnerable. Perhaps emboldened by the events in Iraq and Afghanistan, large protests and riots erupted spontaneously in Iran. Night after night, thousands of people poured out, on foot and in cars, near the campus of Tehran University to shout anti-government slogans. Anti-riot police, Basij, and the regular police were dispatched nightly to battle the unruly crowds, who threw bricks and set fires to keep the cops away.

Student activists were at the forefront of these street demonstrations. For the first time, I heard the roar of "Death to the Dictator," which protestors said was meant for Iran's supreme leader, Ayatollah Ali Khamenei. And then more shocking words: "Mr. Bush, where are you?" Although Iranians did not wish for war, at that early stage of the American occupation of Iraq, when the depth of the fiasco had not yet materialized, many wondered if Iran was missing out on an American-imported democracy and economic prosperity.

I had been quickly dispatched by the *Wall Street Journal* from Baghdad, where I was based, to my childhood hometown, Tehran. In the midst of street battles, speeches, and mass protests, meals (especially those lovingly prepared by my grandmother) had become a refuge for me, stolen moments of normality and appetite in a city where nothing much else seemed normal.

At night, as my cell phone rang with news of riots, clashes, and arrests, my grandmother hovered around me insisting I finish a plate of lamb shank and green rice, made from fresh dill and fava beans, before I headed out the door.

The charged environment of that summer was the backdrop of the student activists' press conference. They wanted to tell us they had canceled their annual campus demonstration in light of recent crackdowns because they were afraid violent clashes would result. They did not suspect what awaited them outside the door that day.

After watching the abduction, I remember feeling shocked and then confused. This wasn't what I was used to seeing in Iran. Yes, dissidents and critics were routinely jailed and tortured, but rarely did the regime put out its iron fist in broad daylight for all to see, in front of a group of foreign journalists. Something was changing. The regime seemed to have acquired a sudden willingness to resort to open violence.

Iran captured the world's attention in the spring of 2009, when millions of people poured into the streets contesting the reelection of President Mahmoud Ahmadinejad. But for those of us who had been covering Iran for decades, the country's downward spiral from the path of reform to dictatorship began that summer of 2003, with the protests and the arrests of students.

On that day, many thoughts ran through my mind: *Is it safe to linger around to gather more information, or should I ditch the scene?* As I pondered, the students who were still inside the building called to us from the window.

"Please don't go. Please come back inside and stay with us. If you leave us they will raid the building and take all of us away," pleaded one of them from the second-floor window.

The students believed that the presence of international journalists would grant them some protection. And so I didn't eat that day. We didn't go to the Artist House Café. I spent nine hours, along with about half a dozen other journalists, acting as human shields to the student activists hiding inside the building. Lunch could wait.

While gunmen waited for us outside, we worked the phones calling reformist Parliament members, the president's office, and Tehran's police chief. Although Iran's shadow power structure allows for Basij to operate independently from the police, we still thought the police chief had the power to intervene. Eventually, teams of police officers were dispatched to escort us out of the area. They told us to head straight home and not stop on the way.

It turned out that our efforts bought the students time, but not safety. In the weeks that followed, nearly every one of the students present at the press conference and the activist leaders with whom I had dined at the Artist House Café would be arrested and jailed. They were picked up, in more or less the same unofficial, brutal manner, by plainclothes men with guns.

At my family's home late at night unable to sleep, I combed through my notebooks, ticking off the names of the detained students. I imagined them confined to tiny cells in solitary confinement at the notorious Evin prison. I wondered how they coped with the lengthy interrogations and the torture they would inevitably face. I felt guilty for quoting them in my stories—even with their consent—and knew those published comments would be used against them in court. When these thoughts became unbearable, I remembered the students' faces as they laughed and drafted speeches about freedom while passing around a bowl of saffron rice pudding, digging in their spoons with delight and insisting that I must have a taste.

I didn't have the heart to go back to the Artist House Café that summer. But on future trips, I did go back. A new generation of student activists, more seasoned and angrier, has emerged, and they still go there to eat lunch and share their dreams of a freer, more democratic Iran over a perfectly delicious dish of walnut and pomegranate stew.

THE OVERSIZE HELMSMAN
OF AN UNDERSIZE COUNTRY
~ISRAEL~

MATT REES

ARIEL SHARON WAS ASHAMED OF HIS WEIGHT. I COULDN'T TELL YOU exactly how heavy he was; the jacket of the light-gray business suit he usually wore disguised the extent of his belly and the dangling mass of his upper arms. Only when he walked could you make out the way he lifted his thighs around each other instead of moving them directly forward.

For the most part, he kept his eating out of the public eye. The first time I saw him in the full of his copious flesh, he occupied a minor ministry in Benjamin Netanyahu's first government. His aides scheduled a photo op on a train, as his ministry happened to be responsible for Israel's piffling rail system. The flacks exchanged a helpless glance as the welcoming railroad officials guided the minister toward the buffet car. "Just for a coffee," he called out to them. And a muffin. And another muffin, too.

It could hardly have mattered less at that time, it seemed. In 1998, Sharon was already seventy years old, and he was generally acknowledged to be finished. He had been the outcast of Israeli politics since the Lebanon War of 1982, when a commission of inquiry found that, as defense minister, he had maneuvered Israel into a disastrous war and, to compound the error, had failed to restrain Israel's Christian allies when they entered the Palestinian refugee camp of Sabra and Shatila to carry out a massacre. When

Netanyahu won election in 1996, he overlooked Sharon, though the old man had been a founder of his Likud Party. Only a protest by a leading party hack persuaded Netanyahu to cobble together a ministry with little apparent power for Sharon. Everyone knew it was just a sop to a man almost no one wanted anymore.

Let him eat cake. Or muffins. Whatever he likes. In fact, let him stuff his face so much he'll keep quiet. That was Netanyahu's formula.

Yet the lack of self-control that overcame Sharon during his Lebanon war and in the face of oily baked goods was never again in evidence when it came to politics. From then until a stroke left him comatose, his was the most predatory and highly focused mind in the Israeli Knesset. He surprised Netanyahu by making his Infrastructure Ministry a focal point for the building of settlements on occupied land and the grabbing, as he put it, of West Bank hilltops in defiance of the peace agreement Israel had signed on the White House lawn in 1993.

Sharon, it turned out, had a political appetite that, for a time, could only be sated by his hunger for Israel to consume the land of the West Bank. Although his body was obese, his mind was more nimble than ever before. He wasn't going to let the United States and Europe hand his precious land on a plate to Yasser Arafat. (Arafat never developed more than a little pot belly, by the way. He mostly ate vegetables and, disturbingly, used to like to shovel wedges of bread and hummus directly into his guests' mouths, while leering at them from a distance most of us would describe as very much inside our personal space.)

As Sharon moved closer to the pinnacle of power, against all the odds, he became more circumspect about food. On several occasions, he even attempted to hide his eating from me.

When I went to see him on his farm in southern-central Israel a few months before he became Israel's prime minister in February 2001, he wasn't wearing the business suit. His gargantuan form was revealed. In his casual shirt and jeans, he looked like Homer Simpson. His bulk was such that he seemed to lack all physical features. I could've drawn him as a single, smooth ellipse from forehead to toe.

Yet he had timed my visit very carefully. As I arrived at Sycamore Farm, the name he gave to the home he'd had since the early 1970s and one of the few private ranches in Israel, he greeted me by saying that I had just missed the breakfast he had shared with his family—one of his sons lived with his wife and kids on the farm, and the other was visiting.

After we had bumped through his cattle herd in a Jeep, stroked a bull that made even Sharon look lightweight, and strolled among his goats, we sat at his kitchen table for an interview. Sharon changed from a plaid shirt into a blue denim shirt that he thought would look better in a portrait photograph with his light-colored eyes. He had even made me hire a makeup artist to cover the patches of liver spotting on his cheeks and scalp. The table remained empty throughout our talk, even when he told me how convivial it was to sit there during the delicious lunches he shared with his family. As noon rolled around, the man they called the Bulldozer came to his feet and said, "Well, it's time for me to have lunch with my family. I'm sorry you can't stay." He reached out for a handshake, which left makeup on my fingers. There'd been liver spots on the back of his hand, too.

I assume he knew that, if I were to be invited to eat with the family, I'd be certain to open my story with that scene. Journalists, after all, like to demonstrate how far they've been allowed into a politician's circle, to show that they're privy to the confidences of the powerful. Compared to a stiff, formal interview, the breaking of bread is the closest one can get to the movers and shakers without breaking ethical rules. Sharon wasn't a third-rate has-been anymore, plucking muffins from the tray of the dining car on the Haifa to Tel Aviv commuter line. He was the leader of the opposition, the man who told me he believed he'd be the next prime minister. The intifada was a few weeks old, and Sharon was one of the first Israelis to identify this conflict not as some kind of Palestinian uprising, but as an existential struggle for the nation's survival. He didn't want people to read articles in which he shoveled down potato salad and devoured chickens whole; didn't want people saying, "Look, it's the same old Sharon, the same old monster with no self-control. He can't stop eating, and he can't stop himself sending tanks here and there. He has no borders, no limits."

So he sent me home before he sat down with his family.

It was okay by me. I never liked to eat with the people I was writing about. It always felt forced. The food, particularly in the Middle East, precludes too much serious talk. I always felt as though I were somehow expected to behave at such meals as if it were a social occasion. But I don't like to socialize with politicians and, after all, they're not my friends. Both sides of the table would be putting on an act. The shared meal strips bare what it's actually supposed to disguise: the fact that the journalist is using the subject for material in an article, and the subject is using the journalist for publicity and the dissemination of a political message. Besides, I don't eat so much, and when I do I like to be relaxed and focused on my food.

I'd have wanted to know what was on the table in Sharon's kitchen; I just wouldn't have wanted to spend all that time grinning stupidly and making small talk with his daughter-in-law.

As I left his home, I thought back to the photos I'd seen of the dashing young commando and general of the 1950s and 1960s. Sharon had been famous then for his relatively long blond hair. A bit of a sex symbol, though he was hardly spare in his build even then. All the stories he told as he looked out of the picture window in the kitchen were romantic tales of early Zionists defying violent Arabs to build a proto-state and along the way finding love. The self-abnegating pioneers presumably had little opportunity to gorge themselves as Sharon did.

I developed a theory, based on the kind of intuition that journalists are supposed to eschew, that the abuse endured by a politician—particularly a controversial politician vilified around the world, who was the main target

of a demonstration by four hundred thousand Israelis in 1982—could lead
to the kind of self-hatred that lies behind many people's overeating.

Friends of Sharon also told me that, while the old man used to let things
slip on outings like the railroad photo op, his wife, Lily, would keep his eating somewhat in check at home. When she died in 2000, he ate to keep his
grief down in his stomach. Perhaps food became a more problematic issue
for him then because, just when he needed her emotional support for the
big push to the country's top job, he also needed her wifely nagging to keep
him from overdoing it at the table.

I continued to write about Sharon during the intifada, when he sent Israeli forces into every Palestinian town and village to snuff out the suicide
bombers. On the way, I happened across still more food lore about him. He
had a penchant for barbecued turkey testicles, which I have since discovered to be a little gummy, much like spine or brain, and to have a slight
savor of scallops. His most favored companions would always report their
conversations to me as having taken place over a meal at the farm. One told
me that, as he called the intifada "a struggle over our existence," Sharon
filled his face with chicken salad.

A former aide noted that Arik, as Israelis call him, believed in coexis-
tence with the Palestinians. As evidence he pointed out that Sharon used to
send his driver to a particularly good roast-chicken restaurant in Beit Jala,
a village on the edge of Bethlehem, to bring back pots of the special garlic
puree made by the owner, a Palestinian Christian.

There were those who thought that Sharon's transformation during his
time as prime minister—from a man condemned as a war criminal to a
rationalist who became the first head of an Israeli government to refer to
the country's presence in the West Bank and Gaza as an "occupation"—was
intended to make the world love him, to replace the images of wailing Palestinians at Sabra and Shatila with the more welcome lamentations—in
the eyes of the world's media, at least—of Israeli settlers booted out of their
colonies in the Gaza Strip in 2005.

It could be that he wanted to be loved, though more likely he saw that holding on to the settlements would lead to inevitable disaster. Israel would soon have found itself ruling over a growing Palestinian population, which is already equal to the number of Jews and will soon represent the majority of the people living in historic Palestine. In other words, Sharon decided to lose the weight represented by the West Bank and Gaza, even though he had done so much to add those extra pounds, so that the skinny little state of Israel—seven miles across at its narrowest point—could live on in good health.

The health of Sharon himself, however, couldn't be salvaged. He suffered a stroke in December 2005 and another in early 2006. The second left him in a permanent vegetative state. Because his health failed him just before he was expected to win a new election with a promise of clearing Israel out of most of the West Bank, Sharon left Israel to linger just as his comatose body would, unable to change course and seemingly drifting toward a doom that could come anytime.

At an interview in his Jerusalem residence shortly before his final stroke, Sharon showed himself once more to be conscious of his physique. It took me an hour to get through the security check at the Balfour Street residence in Rehavia, a neighborhood that passes for "leafy" in most journalistic descriptions, though the trees sporting those leaves are parched if you pause to examine the roots. It wasn't my fault it took so long to get in; *Time* magazine had flown in a photographer, Gillian Laub, who takes portraits with deep chiaroscuro effects and who travels with almost as much lighting equipment as U2 on tour. Each bulb had to be checked, it seemed, so that it couldn't be used to threaten the prime minister.

Once inside the modest official residence of the Israeli prime minister, we sat at a long dark-wood dining table. Gillian attempted to coax Sharon into a portrait shot sitting in front of the table.

"No, I want to stay behind the table," he muttered, hiding his bulky frame—as an aide later confirmed—beneath the tabletop.

While Gillian's shutter clicked, I spoke at length with Sharon, making a considerable effort to focus on his right eye, the one that didn't zip out of control up toward the top of its socket at random moments.

Only when Gillian had finished with her shoot did we move through the small sitting room and into the prime minister's inner sanctum. Alone, except for me and his chief press aide, Sharon relaxed behind his small desk and let his tall black leather office chair rock backward. In the center of the desk, the house staff had placed a plate of small round halva cookies. Israelis offer these with coffee.

When the coffee arrived, Sharon slid the as-yet-untouched plate across the surface of the desk so that it sat in front of him. As we talked, he munched his way through the entire plate of sesame-flavored cookies, which have the texture of a very soft shortbread. The crumbs gathered on his navy blue tie, collecting in a butter-yellow strip on the ledge formed by the protrusion of his belly. He brushed at the crumbs around his mouth, which landed on his lapels.

By this time it was past nine o'clock at night. Apparently Sharon's self-control diminished when he wasn't watched by photographers with the power to record an unflattering image and, like many of us, his tiredness at the end of a demanding day urged an injection of sugar. Quite a lot of sugar. There had been more than a dozen cookies on the plate Sharon emptied.

After I left him that night, I thought about Sharon's gorging. It couldn't truly be called Rabelaisian, because in person—regardless of his bullish political persona—he was the last man one would accuse of impoliteness or gross behavior. In fact, he was rather outlandishly gentlemanly for an Israeli, compared to the uncouth bluntness cultivated by many of his compatriots as an antidote to the manners of the European society that had persecuted them.

I understood the isolation and self-hatred of his overeating, the need to keep the consumption at least from public view, even though his bulk shoved it in their faces after the fact. Politicians all have their secrets. Sharon's successor as prime minister, Ehud Olmert, combed a foot of hair across his obviously bald head. After Olmert came a second term for Netanyahu, who smokes cigars as long as a porno penis, but refuses to be photographed doing so because it's hardly the way a man of the people relaxes. (Netanyahu also turned up frequently at my gym in Jerusalem, marching listlessly on the treadmill as he read digests from aides and making no apparent reduction in his own paunch, which shows signs of one day reaching Sharonian proportions.)

So this was Sharon's secret. He wanted people to think he wasn't fat, when he patently was. Perhaps delusion is part of political success. The nature of elections is that the public chooses to be deluded by politicians. Why shouldn't the politicians deceive themselves, too? A politician must have the kind of ego that refuses to allow him to see himself for who he is. In a conflict zone like Israel, that self-deception might need to be still deeper, because the purported stakes are higher. American politicians ask voters to trust them with their mortgages, their savings, their schools. Israeli politicians tell electors they'd better vote for them or else Israel's enemies may triumph and their state will cease to exist.

I sensed that I couldn't report what I'd learned about Sharon through his eating—not in the kind of magazine for which I used to write. It was too much about feel. It wasn't attributable to some expert in a quote. It wouldn't be balanced, in the way of Middle Eastern reporting, with another expert saying, "To be sure, there are Arab leaders who eat too much, as well."

Since the spring of 2006, when his doctors concluded that he wouldn't recover from his coma, Sharon has lain in a private room in Tel Hashomer, a Tel Aviv hospital with a long-term care facility. The macabre joke among Israeli political correspondents is that no one would recognize him because the doctors aren't overfeeding him through the tube with which he takes his nourishment. So he's down to a normal weight. He's reported to be about 110 pounds.

PART THREE

FOOD UNDER FIRE

SAME-DAY COW
~AFGHANISTAN~

TIM HETHERINGTON

IT WAS COLD AND QUIET UP ON THE ABAS GHAR RIDGE. A FEW CROWS flew overhead and circled back in their quest for food, clearly spotting the American unit that was spread out along the trail below. The men relaxed and talked in hushed voices. It was October 2007, and the soldiers were on the third day of a combat operation aimed at flushing out insurgents in the Korengal Valley—widely considered one of the most deadly places for American soldiers in Afghanistan. Some lay down against their packs while others gathered in small groups, white ribbons of smoke spiraling upward from their cigarettes. The lieutenant was busy on his radio, and many took it as an opportunity to open up an MRE (Meal, Ready-to-Eat) ration pack. Sergeant Stichter sat beside a large tree and focused intently on spreading the contents of a tube of jelly over a beef patty. Sterling Jones watched the culinary experiment and chuckled to himself, "We eat our boredom."

For Staff Sergeant Larry Rougle from Utah, an MRE on the side of the Abas Ghar would be his last meal. Half an hour later, he would be dead and two others wounded, shot at close range after insurgents managed to overrun their position. U.S. intercepts had picked up the enemy whispering on the radios but hadn't realized that this was because they were so close to where the men were camped out. Gunfire exploded around the men, the bullets breaking off branches and tearing up the hillside. Spenser Dunn, in the middle of his meal, lurched forward to find cover behind a pine tree, sending the contents of his ration pack flying. Meanwhile, on an outcrop eighty yards away, Kevin Rice fell back through thick foliage after being shot through the stomach. The ambush was over in an instant, leaving behind it the debris of spilled rations and a trail of blood down the mountainside.

Napoleon famously said that an army marches on its stomach. Likewise today, American soldiers in Afghanistan live and die on MREs. Meals, Ready-to-Eat, otherwise known as Meals Rejected by Everyone, Meals Rarely Edible, Meals Rejected by the Enemy, or Materials Resembling Edibles. While five thousand soldiers in rear bases wear pressed clothing and feast on fresh produce, front-line combat soldiers in their alternative reality hold company with fleas and the thick chocolate plastic packaging of MRE meal packs. Field rations for combat units originated by order of Congress during the American Revolutionary War and have undergone numerous incarnations since—most recently from the heavy-duty canned rations of the Korean War to the "Meal, Combat, Individual" ration (also known as C-rations or Charlie Rats) of the Vietnam War, to the introduction of dehydrated MREs in the early 1980s.

Inevitably soldiers have a complicated relationship with their rations, which they both malign and fetishize. They ascribe all sorts of powers to these hated, beloved meals. Some claim the MREs contain dangerous levels of bromide designed to take away their sex drive (though judging by the amount of porn I saw consumed in the Korengal, this hadn't worked); others that the gum provided in each packet is really a laxative (though I once went through four packets without finding relief from a terrible bout of constipation). It is even commonly held that "Charms"—the hard-boiled candies that come with one of the meals—are, by their very name, harbingers of bad luck. Whenever someone found a packet of Charms in his MRE in the Korengal, it was customary for him to hurl the candies down the mountainside. I imagined how young Korengali children might come across the American treats lodged between boulders as they tended their goats and cows on the slopes below. Specialist Cortez looked a little sheepish one day when he was caught red-handed eating a whole packet. He immediately confessed to premeditation—claiming he was so bored out of his mind that he had wanted to start a firefight by eating them when no one was looking. It didn't work.

In the upside-down world of the Korengal, eating was a way to beat the boredom that suffocated soldiers between bouts of fighting. Later on during my many weeks with the soldiers there, I'd wonder what it was about food up there—it wasn't that you stopped caring about eating, but it was hard to derive any satisfaction from an MRE. The name of each meal would change, but the contents seemed the same.

Whatever the intentions of the Department of Defense, its rations did not provide any emotional fulfillment—there was rarely a moment of satisfied reverie after eating an MRE during which a soldier's guard might drop. Certainly U.S. MREs did not replicate the European army experience of a carefully crafted *gastronomie*—French ration packs assumed a satisfying meal by the very inclusion of an after-dinner cigarette. Some of the best meals out there had little to do with what was actually being eaten, and more to do with the context and act of eating itself: Specialist Jason Monroe (a.k.a. "Money") working his way through two pounds of canned tuna that a relative had sent him in a care package, in an act of defiant excess.

While emotional satisfaction may not have been possible, just thinking about those brown packets could nevertheless evoke a Pavlovian response, especially on the final stretch of a patrol. You needed to pay attention during the sprint out of the village of Kalaygal—it would be careless to get shot after getting up so early and doing all the hard work—but once around the cusp of the spur, the final two hundred yards back to Outpost Restrepo were plain sailing. Situated on a high rocky outcrop with commanding views over the Korengal, Restrepo was an important strategic piece in the battle for the valley. The final moments of the steep climb up to the outpost required little concentration, and my mind often strayed to thoughts of food.

Looking out across the way one morning as I passed through the concertina wire, I could see tall trees dotting the upper reaches of valley walls, their silhouettes standing against the morning light, while down on the valley floor, a blanket of mist thinned to reveal small patchworks of yellow and green terrace. Local people were bent over gathering ripe bundles of wheat, and small flecks were cattle meandering across the rocky crags in search of a morning meal. I found my colleague Sebastian already sitting down on a small rocky outcrop that serves as a kind of bench. He was shaking his head from side to side, and then, tilting his head back, finally took a large gulp.

"I'm just having a coffee," he said. "I lost the cup, so I'm just putting the coffee mix in my mouth and adding water." He paused, noticing my expression.

"It's actually not that bad," he said.

It has been many months since I was last in the Korengal, but I still can't entirely shake the effects of living off processed, indigestible material for months on end. As much as the fighting, the daily ritual of eating became a fundamental part of the experience we all shared. Nowadays I go out to a fancy restaurant in New York and will sit there like some confused old person wondering what to eat, but out in the Korengal I moved fast at mealtimes. I knew I'd have only a split second to get to the scrambled eggs and ham pouch when someone opened up the holy grail of MREs—the luminous white box of winter's rations.

Unlike the brown boxes of regular MREs, the white boxes for winter food contained freeze-dried meals that required the addition of hot water. It was actually like making a meal. Even if you were in the middle of wiping a dry cracker with a healthy dose of jalapeño cheese spread, the sweet music of someone ripping open a new carton of food was the signal to get off your ass and over there before the rest of the marauding hordes beat you to the best stuff. Bobby Gene had large square paws that could easily beat me to the bottom of the box in search of Beef Ravioli. No point in hesitating—I mean, who wants to end up with the loser's lot of Cheese Macaroni—not even the platoon dog was that stupid.

To pick the right MRE packet, one needed to comprehend in a split second all the ramifications of a particular choice. Each meal packet was its own universe, with its own particular assets and liabilities. For instance, take the packet Chicken Fajitas. In 2007, the *Salt Lake Tribune* asked three gourmet chefs to taste eighteen different MRE meals. All survived the experiment and went on to draw up a ranking table to compare their experiences. On a tasting scale of 1 to 10, the average of all the meals was a miserable 5.7, but the Chicken Fajitas was singled out as being the worst of all, ranking only an average score of 1.3. Framed like this, you'd think every soldier would avoid choosing an MRE Chicken Fajitas—but in fact, there were plenty of reasons why this would be a good choice. Think about all the great things that came in the brown sack of deliciousness along with the fajitas. I remember an orange beverage far superior to the fluorescent pink grapefruit one that came with another main course and stained your teeth. And there were chewy Tootsie Rolls that you could sequester away in your personal food treasury for a later date; syrupy spiced apples; and the pièce de résistance—cherry cobbler that could be warmed up. Each MRE was more than just the main course by which it was known; it was a holistic experience.

Army logisticians determined that soldiers should eat only MREs no longer than twenty-one days in a row, but Outpost Restrepo became some kind of weird laboratory where men were pitted against the laws of nature and evolved new eating habits. One day I came across Sergeant Aron Hijar in the midst of culinary experimentation. In one hand he held an open packet of Meatloaf and Gravy, while in his other he slowly ground a pile of crackers in his palm and added them to the mixture. Next, a tube of peanut butter spread went in, followed by a sprinkling of M&M's candies rounded off with two mini-bottles of Tabasco sauce. Hijar stirred the potent mixture together with a brown plastic spoon while staring at me intently.

"You're not going to heat that up?" I asked.

"Warm food is for pussies," he replied emphatically. "This is how we used to eat at Ranger School. They never gave us enough time to eat, and when you did have time, you were so tired that this was the easiest way to eat so you could get to sleep as quickly as possible. Just mash it all up and shovel it down."

"Looks fucking disgusting," I said.

"Looks can be deceptive," he replied.

For a lucky few, there was life beyond the MRE. Those based down with Battle Company's headquarters element at the main outpost on the valley floor had access to the company's two cooks—Bui and Lackley. Both were important fixtures in the life of the company, though it was misleading to use the word *cook* to describe their work. In fact, Bui was so compromised by his obsession with Gameboy that I'm not sure which was worse—having to eat what he served at the main outpost, or resigning oneself to a life of MREs at one of the more remote outposts like Restrepo.

One day, the men up at Restrepo reached what could be called an MRE breaking point. I was not there at the time, but Sergeant Brendan O'Byrne, from Pennsylvania, told me the story later. It began when Sergeant Al and Hoyt had a crazy idea.

"Hey, let's kill a fucking cow!" one of them said.

Some cattle had been grazing close to Outpost Restrepo, and the men had one eye out for the herders who normally accompanied them. Often the enemy would send people toward the outpost to scout for soft spots in the base's defense—and what better pretext than looking for a wandering cow? On this particular day, though—one of those long, quiet days in the valley when the fighting had died down for lack of ammunition rather than will—no one seemed to be around. The herd clung precipitously to the loose slate ground, the cows whisking their tails and oblivious to the men peering down from the green sand-bagged roof of the armory bunker.

As luck would have it, Lackley happened to be visiting from the main outpost that lay three thousand feet below on the valley floor. He'd come up to Restrepo on the pretense of bringing up supplies, but in reality he wanted to get into a firefight so he could earn his Combat Infantryman's Badge—known simply as a CIB. A posting to the Korengal was considered dangerous enough, but Restrepo—being the outpost closest to enemy territory—was the tip of the spear in the company effort in the valley, and a visit there would guarantee even a cook his CIB. So when Lackley staggered up, sweating and out of breath, everyone in the platoon was happy to see he'd made the long hike up to their flea-infested home—it was, at the very least, a gesture of camaraderie that they welcomed. They ended up taking him on a patrol down to the village of Kalaygal and stayed long enough to ensure they'd get shot at on the way out—so Lackley was able to get himself in a fight and rightfully claim his medal. Content with the outcome—no one was killed and everyone had a good laugh—he stayed up for a couple more days, sunbathing with the rest of them while they waited for the enemy to get an ammunition resupply.

Now, looking down on the cattle, Lackley suggested that if they killed a cow, he'd cook it up on the makeshift grill with some of the onions he'd brought up. It was decided that they couldn't shoot it—a gunshot would raise the alarm down at the main base that Restrepo was under attack—so Hoyt decided to make a spear out of a tent pole and a Rambo knife, attaching it with parachute cord and some gaffer tape. They picked out a fat brown cow that had made the fatal mistake of straying too close to the concertina wire and encircled it on one side, trapping it between them and the wire. O'Byrne told me how Hoyt got close enough to stab it a few times, gouging it in the neck—the poor beast went down without much of a fight, bleeding out on the mountainside. The men rolled the body down the incline and dragged it quickly inside the perimeter of the outpost, looking around to make sure no one—officer or Afghan—had seen them. Once inside, no one knew exactly what to do next, so they decided to take its head off first with a Christmas tree saw. This didn't work too well, until Murphy started twisting the head around. It snapped off and sent him sliding down the mountainside. Everyone roared with laughter while O'Byrne—who had no butchering experience whatsoever—stood nearby giving authoritative instructions as they sliced it down the belly, taking care to avoid the bladder. They cut themselves the tenderest steaks the cow had to offer. Finally Lackley rubbed his hands and took to the grill. Minutes later the men relished what became known as "same-day cow."

About a week later, some local people came looking for a cow they claimed was missing from their herd.

"We had buried it and burned it and stuff like that, and we didn't have a clue how this guy knew we'd killed his cow," O'Byrne told me. "So we were like, 'Nah, we didn't kill your cow.' Finally Sergeant Patterson said, 'Listen, your cow got caught in the C-wire. We didn't kill your cow.' They wanted money for it, and we were like, 'We'll give you some rice and beans and stuff that equals the same value of your cow, but we're not giving you money for the cow.' They all got pissed off at us. I heard the estimate was ten thousand dollars that we had to give the Afghanis for the cow. But that was the best steak I ever had."

EAU DE CADAVRE
~SOMALIA AND RWANDA~

SAM KILEY

HIS SHARPLY HONED NOSE AND CHEEKBONES ARE SET IN GUNMETAL
skin and framed against a chalk background. The white tips of his incisors
are sneaking a look from beneath enigmatic lips. His eyes are a mass of
blue-green. The boy is statue-still, and beautiful.

The slide projector clatters to the next image. It is a wide-angle photograph of the same boy, taken on the same day by me in Baidoa in 1992. I've
composed this with no sense of irony, just of horror. The lad, no more than
ten, is lying on his back with his arms flung out next to two others, both of
them in their late teens. They're all skeleton-thin because they're dead of
starvation. Their eyes are green with bluebottle flies.

We'd picked up ninety bodies that morning on the Death Bus. That is
what the locals, who lived in the dusty town about a hundred miles inland
from Mogadishu, called it. Families who'd drifted in from the wide alluvial
plains on either side of the Jubba River had lost their food stocks to bandits
who'd been organised by warlords. Now, destitute, they propped themselves
against mud walls and waited for the bus. They all wore dirty white shrouds.
Some curled in the thin shade of thorn trees by the roadside. They were
almost all going to be passengers. Local businessmen organised the bus, a
jangling truck with a roaring diesel engine, to pick them up and take them

out of town for burial. They were slung into a long open trench cut into a field stubbly with harvested sorghum stalks.

I'd clambered around on the bus since it started its route at dawn. Just one aid organization had turned up at this time, run by a saintly Irish nurse. Her little wattle-ringed camp was becoming a magnet for the starving, who wobbled silently toward it out of the dust beyond. She had food only for kids—adults turned, without protest, from her gates to sit and wait for the bus.

I swung like a monkey from the shiny worn metal piping of the frame over the back of the truck, seeking odd angles for my pictures. I was twenty-eight. I'd seen plenty of war in Ethiopia and during the civil war in Mogadishu by then. Bodies were nothing new to me, but I burned with an urge to "do something." Sometimes journalists get the chance to feel that what they tell the world about what's happening in the world might actually change it. This was my chance, our chance (I was not alone). And so I took the pictures, hiding behind the lens. I tried to compose images that, while they were of dead people, might be publishable somewhere. I worried that they might offend and therefore be ignored.

The bus dumped its passengers in the stubbly field, not far from the road south of Baardheere, and headed back into town. It hit the main road that went left to Kenya and right to Mogadishu. I banged on the roof of the cab to stop the driver opposite a pastel-pink building with hand-painted advertisements for spaghetti and long bars of Sunlight soap.

"Thanks," I called to the driver, giving his door a grateful pat. Then I clapped my hands together and said out loud, "Fuck me, I'm starving."

Nothing inflames the appetite like a famine. And there was always plenty of food in Somalia during the mass starvation that killed about 350,000 people. That's why, in the end, the United States led the world's first humanitarian military intervention. Warlords were starving their own people to death and charging the international community to feed them. It was the world's biggest, and most blatant, protection racket. George Bush

Senior smashed it. He saved many thousands of lives, even if things went bad in the end with the "Black Hawk down" debacle.

As journalists stationed in Mogadishu's Green Zone, covering the war, famine, intervention, and mayhem in Somalia, we never lacked for food. Over dinners of endless lobster in the Al Sahafi Hotel we talked about anything but our work; we talked as if we were stoned, and some were. We got sick of lobster, which was abundant off the coast of Mogadishu. The means to get it to market in Europe had been sunk or stolen by the Somalis—so we scoffed lobster till we gagged.

We learned to eat spaghetti with one hand, curling it between little and index fingers back and forth until a ball of it could be popped into the mouth. Camel steak was delicious, and it often came sitting on a pile of spaghetti. We ate and swam at a bullet-riddled shack called the Indian Ocean Club. It was on the edge of the Green Zone, where fighting had turned the city centre into concrete lace. In short breaks between covering the fighting, Dan Eldon, my photographer friend who was soon murdered by an enraged Somali mob, and I leaped in and out of the waves. We padded to the club across white sand to guzzle prawns stewed in coconut milk, saffron, tamarind, and cumin. We sluiced it down with nose-achingly cold beer. We stopped swimming when we realised we were down-current from the local abattoir and UN soldiers started getting bitten in half by sharks. One even took an armed Moroccan soldier in full combat gear, including flak jacket, from a rock like a trout taking a grasshopper off a leaf.

Old Etonian, cameraman, and former mujahideen guerrilla Carlos Mavroleon made a big deal out of teaching me to make peperoncino aglio e olio. He made it sound like I was being initiated into a brotherhood of culinary superiors. Carlos had a gentle, fey voice like a pantomime homosexual. He also carried a Colt 45 pistol hidden under his shirt. Ordinarily journalists who carry guns are freaks and fantasists likely to get themselves killed. Carlos was different.

"If I knew that all you were going to do was fry up some garlic in olive oil with snipped-up chilli, I'd have stayed on the roof drinking with everyone else. This is bollocks," I said, giving his shoulder a gentle shove.

It was exquisite. But I haven't cooked it since Carlos was found dead in a Peshawar hotel room in 1998.

For the young and brash among us, these were the good days. We had war. We had famine. We had two seasons in the sun. We also had good food, plenty of booze, freshly made watermelon juice with a hint of ginger, little perfumed mangoes from Afgooye, and rooms fumigated against bugs with frankincense and myrrh. Enough of us got killed to make the rest feel brave and noble.

Rwanda was different.

I was smuggled in from neighbouring Burundi by Vjeko Ćurić, a Franciscan monk who was Rwanda's Scarlet Pimpernel. We drove in his small Toyota saloon. We were stopped at a roadblock by *interahamwe* killers. One wore a doctor's white coat with a stethoscope around his neck. We were about ten miles short of Gitarama, not far from Vjeko's parish. The white coat was splattered with fresh blood. A woman in a purple dress was lying facedown. The naked soles of her feet rested on the edge of the tarmac. I could see her white knickers. Her head was in the ditch with a tangle of three or four other bodies.

We had passed a corpse about every ten yards for miles behind us as we'd driven north from the border with Burundi. This was early May 1994. The genocide in Rwanda was three weeks old, but no one had quite dared to use the word—*genocide*. In those days this was a big thing to say. Today it's hard to find a conflict in which the term isn't chucked about.

A million people were killed in Rwanda in ninety days. We know the numbers because we know how many Tutsis were in the country, and how many survived. Then add in the Hutu moderates, who were the first to die in this perfectly organised state-sponsored mass slaughter, and a million is the minimum figure. That's 11,111 a day—by hand, by machete, with clubs made from the roots of saplings. Many were burned alive. The lucky ones were shot—but had to pay for the privilege in advance. Those with money could die with their children in one burst.

The roadblock "doctor" shoved his bald head into the Toyota and rotated it so he was nose-to-nose with Vjeko. He shouted something in Kinyarwanda, straight into the priest's face. Vjeko laughed and spoke back harshly, then pushed the doc's head back out of the car. We drove on.

I had only understood the guy shouting "Belge? Belge?"

"He wanted to know if you are Belgian. He said if you are then I must hand you over to be butchered. I said, 'No—he's not Belgian, you fool. Look, he's skinny—he doesn't eat enough chips to be Belgian.' Sometimes you just have to scare the morons and murderers."

At Kivumu Vjeko put me up in his parish house. It was a quadrangle of red brick classrooms overhung by a mango tree. His small cell, and small kitchen, opened onto the slab-stone path. He was hiding dozens of Tutsis in a nearby barn and was planning to smuggle them out of the country. I didn't visit them because he said he was being spied on. There were three bullet holes in his kitchen, one above the stove, one through the door frame, another through the foam back of an old armchair. Someone had come to kill him the week before and missed. He'd pushed past them and hidden in the mango tree.

He made a thick bean stew, which we flavoured with chillis. No one wanted to eat meat in Rwanda—not with the sweet grilled-pork smell hanging in the air. Our guts and throats knew it before our minds could recognise the scent of burned human. No one I know who was in Rwanda then can eat roast pork or, worse still, fry chops—they smell of death.

I hired a Mitsubishi Pajero in Burundi and set out northward across the country with a photographer, Dominic Cunningham-Reid. By the time we got to Rusomo Falls, a cascade of chocolate water where the Akagera River separates Rwanda from Tanzania before snaking northeast into Lake Victoria, a few weeks later, I had become used to drinking tea that smelled of dead bodies. The water, every body of water, had a body in it. The rivers, creeks, household cisterns, outdoor shit houses, ponds, and lakes were crammed with corpses. I learned pretty quickly to tell the time of death by the smell of the dead. At Rusomo I walked past a pile of thousands of machetes dropped by Hutu killers who had fled retribution for exile in Tanzania. Standing on the bridge they had taken to safety, I looked down. I timed the number of bodies that tumbled over the falls and floated north—there was one every second. They slopped over the rocks, snagged briefly, and slid on, like Tuscan bean soup being poured from a saucepan. Some of the bodies were brown, some white. Black people bleach white when they've been dead in the water for a few days. We called Rwanda's uniquely horrible water *eau de cadavre*.

By the time I got to Rusomo, I was also starving. I didn't want to drink the tea. And the Tutsi-dominated Rwandan Patriotic Front, which was by then sweeping the Hutu genocidaires out of the country into Tanzania and Zaire, would not allow us to capture and kill any of the hundreds of thousands of goats and chickens that were running feral now that their owners were in mass graves or slopping around in the rivers. Instead, we got a plastic plate of paraffin-flavoured rice every day. I had long ago eaten the round of cured sausage and flat bread I'd brought with me and was feeling weak with hunger, my jeans falling off my hips.

Fruit. We were allowed to pick ripe fruit. Actually, once I lost my temper, leaped out of the car, and ran into a homestead where papayas were dangling like huge green and orange gonads from the tops of rubbery-looking trees. I made Dominic get a long stick.

"You gently poke them out of the tree, I'll catch them before they hit the ground. It will be a doddle—did I ever tell you I played county-level cricket as a wicket keeper when I was at school?" I said.

"Yup," Dom said and dislodged a fruit, which dropped about ten feet, smoothly falling into my cradling hands.

He popped another couple off, and we got into a swinging routine of harvest. I handed them to a Tutsi rebel fighter who had been hitching a ride with us. He piled them gently on the grass. I looked up. Dom dislodged another, which teetered and dropped through a drooping umbrella of leaves—where I lost it.

The sickly-sweet fruit hit me square on the bridge of my nose, burst all the way down my body, and left me coated in pulpy orange flesh and gelatinous seed, which looked like frogspawn and smelled of vomit. The Tutsi fighter, Leon, spluttered. Laughter did not come easily to him; his family had been murdered a month earlier. But now an orange *mzungu* (white man) was standing before him. None of us had washed for three weeks and we reeked. (I would spend the rest of the week stinking of puke. I would attract swarms of flies that hatched in the flesh of the dead.) Leon walked away from us so that he could laugh discreetly. He even covered his face with his hands. Then he returned to where we were now carving up the unexploded fruit on the bonnet of the Pajero.

"I wish you'd let us grab a chicken. Why not, just this time? They're just running about."

"They belong to someone," he told me. I didn't state the obvious, but I thought it: *But Someone, everyone, is dead.*

We didn't make that mistake again in Rwanda. For our next trip, Dom and I brought kit bags heaving with instant meals, tinned sardines, tuna and fruit. We found half-litre bottles of Tabasco sauce and padded the whole lot with toilet paper and baby wipes. The latter we used to clean our bodies every day so we would never have to get into the water, which stank. We filled the back of the car with 200 litres of petrol, jericans of water, and camping gear. We forgot machetes for cutting firewood—they gave us the creeps anyway, since they were the principal tool of the genocide. Still, it was fun to set off back into Rwanda properly equipped. We were so excited about our provisioning and gear that we stopped thinking about where we were going.

For three weeks we crisscrossed the country, mostly among the *interahamwe* while they continued their killing. They thought we were French commandos, who had been on their side during earlier fighting with the Tutsi-dominated RPF. When the French sent commandos to intervene in Operation Turquoise, which we mistook initially as an effort to stop the mass killing and which turned out to be an attempt to stop the Tutsi advance, French commandos we came across thought we were British special forces. It was bizarre, but true, that the Brits were still the original enemy for the French, and so they felt it was a good idea to keep us "SAS men" close by and under their eyes.

The genocidaires had the backing of the French because the Tutsi rebels spoke English, a legacy of their time in exile in neighbouring Uganda. It seems incredible that the French would give a damn—but they did. They were complicit in genocide, and even today known mass killers remain at large in France, although most French reporters now acknowledge that this was as dark a period in their history as Vichy. When I discovered the last three thousand Tutsis left alive in Rwanda in Bisesero, close to Lake Kivu, the French forces were flying biscuits to the *interahamwe,* who looked down on hillsides strewn with the carcasses of their victims. The *interahamwe* had been killing Tutsis in these hills just the day before and wanted to finish the job. The French had no idea where they were or what had occurred, they just thought they were going to stop the Tutsi advance. By the end of the morning, though, they had been shamed into helping the Tutsis by French colleagues with me, who freaked out when we found a Tutsi girl of about ten. She stood before us wearing a plastic bag on her head; the top of her skull had been opened like an egg by a Hutu militiaman with a machete, who at the time was no doubt guzzling the biscuits the French commandos had flown in.

A week or so later Dom and I were with the French commandos when they rescued Theoneste Bagasora, founder of the *interahamwe,* from the Butare airfield as the Tutsi forces encircled the city. It was many years be-

fore Bagasora was sentenced to life in prison at the International Criminal
Tribunal for Rwanda, convicted of genocide and crimes against humanity.
He was Rwanda's Himmler, the author of the final solution to the "Tutsi
problem." When the French special forces flew out of Butare with Bagasora
in a light aircraft, we were left on the ground, in danger of being trapped
between the advancing Tutsis and the defeated Hutus.

So we drove south, back down the road I'd first travelled with Vjeko two
months earlier. We shot past terrified Hutu government soldiers and got to
the border a few moments before sunset. In central Africa, night falls almost instantly at six every evening. We'd again run out of food. The adrenaline in our systems was causing us stomach cramps, acid was gnawing at
our insides as we drew up outside a Hutu police post and parked about one
hundred yards short of the officers, who were listening to radio reports of
the fall of Butare. They were drinking heavily.

"Monsieur. Monsieur. Can you help me?" a voice whispered in French
from the darkness behind us.

I turned to see a tall, slender, good-looking and well-dressed boy of about
nineteen. He was wearing a designer shirt made of quadrants of different-
coloured cloth, jeans, and running shoes. He looked like a kid from New York.
He was shaking and staring into my eyes. He was a Tutsi—a couple hundred
yards away from safety in Burundi.

"Dom—you're fluent in Swahili, and we're starving. Will you go and ask
the guards if we can buy one of their goats—tell them they can have the liver,
whatever, just keep them drinking and talking. I'll stick with our new friend."

We all walked toward the guards, with Dom shouting Swahili greetings as
we approached. I kept the boy away from them, on my right, so that he could
run into the bush, or dive into the river that marked the border, if they came
for him. Dom is tall, with long blond hair that hangs below his ears. He has
very long arms. He threw them wide in greeting. He swept all the guards
into their little hut as we walked past. I noticed their bloodied machetes lean-
ing against the weatherboard walls.

"Fuck off to Burundi, you cockroach!" one of the guards yelled at our backs. We both froze, then run-walked until we got to the bridge, where I shoved him hard into no-man's-land.

"Oui," I shouted after him. "Fuck off."

I turned back to the guards and Dom. He was speaking such fast and elegant Swahili that they had lost interest in the *inyenzi* (cockroach). Now they were trying to screw Dom for fifty dollars for a kid goat.

"You've got to kill it and clean it for that kind of money," said Dom.

He was haggling with a man of about forty who had bulging eyes. His face was wet with drunken sweat. The whites of his eyes were yellow. The goat was pulled along on a thin bit of string. The policeman had his machete across his knees. He chuckled.

Thwack.

In a lazy, well-practised motion, he took its head clean off.

EATING MUD CRABS IN KANDAHAR

~AFGHANISTAN~

CHRISTINA LAMB

THE ROAD TO MY FIRST ENCOUNTER WITH AFGHAN CUISINE STARTED, oddly enough, at the bar at the American Club in Peshawar, Pakistan. There's always a favorite watering hole for journalists covering a war, and for those reporting on the Soviet occupation of Afghanistan in the 1980s it was this two-story house in University Town.

Frankly, there wasn't much choice. Alcohol was banned in Pakistan, so there were no bars and just a few hotels where you could sign a form to say you were a heathen and a furtive waiter would appear at the door bearing a basket. Inside, under layers of pink napkins and newspaper, would be a bottle of Murree beer brewed by Parsis in Rawalpindi.

The American Club was far more convivial. If only we had realized, Osama bin Laden was living just a few blocks away; but in those days in the 1980s we had never heard of him. The Arab Afghans, as they were known, were mostly people their own countries wanted to get rid of—sinister, shadowy figures who fought like crazy and of whom the Afghan mujahideen were wary at best.

On the menu at the club were cheeseburgers with forbidden bacon and wondrous calorie-laden things that I had never encountered in England, such as sloppy joes and Oreo-cookie ice cream, paid for with tear-off paper coupons bought in five-dollar booklets. To wash them down you could order anything from ice-cold Budweisers to Johnny Walker Black Label.

I was twenty-one when I went to the club for the first time, having set out for the Afghan frontier to be a foreign correspondent. Men were seated in a row at the bar wearing green army jackets, some with old bloodstains or charred bullet holes. As I walked in, a couple of them swiveled around and looked me up and down.

"How many wars have you covered?" asked one in a thick American drawl.

"None, it's my first," I replied nervously.

They were Vietnam vets and could tell me how many Americans had been killed there—58,000—and therefore how many Russians must be killed in Afghanistan. It was simple Cold War arithmetic, and the war they were covering seemed black-and-white—the evil commies versus the noble (Western-backed and -equipped) Afghans. I preferred thinking of it in more romantic David versus Goliath terms of the brave man from the mountains with an old Lee-Enfield rifle and rope sandals ranged against the most powerful army on earth.

Neither, of course, was true. Afghanistan is known as the graveyard of empires, having never been conquered from Alexander the Great to the British. However, the real decisive factor was not the Afghans' tenacious fighting but their CIA-supplied Stinger missiles, which could down Soviet helicopters and thus nullified the advantage of airpower.

Yet when I started questioning the received opinion about the mujahideen, writing about some of their own excesses, I found myself denounced as a commie and eventually banned from the American Club, deprived of beer and pork products. Instead I spent my evenings with Pakistani or Afghan friends or other renegades drinking Russian vodka we called Gorbachev, bought at the local smugglers' market.

I had gone to the club because I desperately wanted to know what foreign correspondents actually did and how they operated. My only experience was a summer as an intern at the *Financial Times,* where foreign correspondents known as the Camel Corps wafted in from exotic destinations, speaking in strange languages on the phones and lugging battered leather satchels of foreign newspapers.

I also wanted information about getting into Afghanistan. I had met a diplomat from the British embassy who I guessed was a spook; he advised me, "Make sure you take your own cup; you can catch all sorts of diseases from the mujahideen." I had never thought about hygiene as part of war reporting and, twenty years on, have never traveled with my own cup.

Like all journalists in Peshawar, I spent all my time trying to get what we called "inside." The way to do this was through one of the resistance parties. Pakistan's military intelligence, ISI, which was in charge of distributing weapons, had followed the old British principle of divide and rule to form seven different groups, most headed by former Kabul university professors.

Some were a waste of time trying. The fundamentalists like Yunus Khalis, a fierce seventy-year-old with a sixteen-year-old wife, and Gulbuddin Hekmatyar, whose men threw acid in the faces of Afghan women who worked, were never going to take along a female journalist. Hekmatyar had me thrown out of an interview because, his men said, he could see my ankles.

Some were hard to take seriously, such the National Islamic Front of Afghanistan (NIFA), run by Pir Gailani and his sons, who had lived in Knightsbridge. We nicknamed them the Gucci muj because of their fondness for neatly pressed camouflage with pens made from gold-plated AK-47 bullets peeping from their top pockets.

Others were too keen—Jamiat-e Islami, run by Professor Rabbani, was so adroit at taking journalists along that I dubbed their office Mujahideen Resistance Tours Ltd. Their favorite tour was to take journalists to the city of Khost, which was not far across the border. I lost count of the number of times I read stories on the "battle for Khost"—it was how we knew there was a newcomer in town who had fallen for their line.

The best plan, it seemed to me, was to get to know individual commanders. Each day I would spend hours sitting awkwardly cross-legged on the floor drinking green tea and crunching sugared almonds from tiny glass dishes. My favorite was Abdul Haq, the twinkly-eyed Kabul commander who was always jovial despite having lost a foot to a land mine and with whom I shared a fondness for pink ice cream.

Once I'd convinced them I wouldn't be a liability, commanders would send me into Afghanistan with their men, disguised as a mujahideen clad in men's baggy pajama trousers secured with a long cord and a woollen cap and dirt rubbed into my fair skin to darken it. The Pashtun honor code would ensure my safety—one fighter would be designated responsible for me and instructed that if anything happened he would be chopped into little pieces.

After all the hassle and anxiety of getting in, the first day in Afghanistan was always wonderful. There was no sign of a border, because there wasn't really one—just a random line, drawn up by the British, which split tribes and villages in half. But the mujahideen always claimed even the air was different, and when I was traveling with them so it seemed.

Even so, once I'd been inside Afghanistan a few days I would dream of getting out. This was less because of the hazards of war, such as being bombed by Soviet helicopters or driving over a mine, but more because there was nothing to eat. My first morning waking up in Afghanistan after a long trek by foot and mule, sitting uncomfortably astride a consignment of RPGs, was high up on a mountain in Paktika. Breakfast, served to me sitting on a roof in the cool, crisp air, was delicious thick cream and warm, floppy, freshly cooked naan. But it was a misleading introduction. Never again did I have such a breakfast. Afghans could survive weeks on nothing but dried naan.

Later a correspondent friend, Marie Colvin, and I made up what we called the War Correspondents Diet. Basically you would eat what you liked for weeks at home, then spend weeks of near-starvation trekking up and down mountains in Afghanistan or some other godforsaken conflict zone.

After I had lived in Peshawar for a while, I met a man called Hamid
Karzai, who was spokesman for the Afghan National Liberation Front headed
by Professor Mojadiddi. The ANLF was a standing joke among Afghans
because it had so few forces inside the country, so hardly any journalists
came to speak to Karzai. This I discovered was a shame, as he was eloquent
and passionate about his country's history—in fact, I had never met anyone
so fiercely proud of his country. He was also a gracious host. His house was
always full of tribal elders from southern Afghanistan whom he had to feed
and shelter. His was an important family—his father was leader of the
Popolzai, one of the royal Durrani tribes—but his brothers had all moved
to America, where they ran Afghan restaurants. Hamid probably served up
more food than they did—being the only representative of the family in
Peshawar, he was expected to provide huge platters of stewed mutton and
colorful pilau rice topped with grated carrots and raisins. For me he always
had some English chocolate.

Karzai's hometown was Kandahar, which he pronounced with a long *a*
in the first syllable that somehow captured his yearning for the place and its
summer winds, which swept across the desert with such a blast of heat it
was said that they could fry a fish. "That's the real Afghanistan," he would
say as told me of its orchards, which grew forty types of grapes and pome-
granates that shone like rubies and had a taste so exquisite they would
bring tears to the eyes.

Early on in our friendship, he decided he was going to take me there.
Eventually in the summer of 1989 we set off, stopping first in Quetta, a
small earthquake-prone town in western Pakistan surrounded by mountains that looked like swirled toffee and seemed to be on the very edge of
the earth. Our first stop was a bazaar full of men with dark eyeliner and
jeweled sandals with high heels, many of whom were holding hands. In
a small shack away from prying eyes, I was kitted out in *shalwar kameez*
and a long length of black silky cotton with fine white stripes that both the

shopkeeper and Karzai could whisk into a turban with a twist of the fingers but I found impossible to tie.

As always with trips to Afghanistan, the journey was delayed for days before starting in a great hurry in the dawn hours, followed by endless waiting. Before leaving town we changed vehicles five times, which as far as I could see just drew more attention to ourselves.

The sun was setting by the time we ended up in a Mitsubishi Pajero heading out of town, climbing the Khojak Pass. All around us desert mountains rose smudged and Sphinxlike and the road passed back-and-forth tunnels for an astonishing switchback train track that British engineers had built. Apart from us the only traffic was a procession of jingle trucks with gaudily painted scenes of luscious Pashtun beauties and Swiss mountain views on their panels, which hid secret compartments for smuggling, the main local industry in this frontier region.

Our companions were Abdul Razzak, one of Kandahar's leading commanders, known as the Airport Killer for his daring raid on the air base used by the Soviets, and Ratmullah, a chubby junior commander with a bushy black beard and eyes as dark as coal yet twinkling with mischief.

It was almost midnight by the time we reached the border, to be greeted by the red flares of heavy guns from nearby Spin Boldak, which the mujahideen were trying to capture. We drove into a compound, and to my surprise the first thing I saw was a calendar on the wall from which stared out the unmistakable face of Yunus Khalis with his henna-orange beard. I couldn't imagine Karzai and Khalis having much in common. "Parties don't matter here," explained Karzai.

Several men emerged swathed in shawls and there was the usual long, guttural exchange of Pashto greetings—how are you, how is your father, what about your father's father, and so on. Then a rose-patterned vinyl tablecloth was spread on the dirt floor and the men sat around it, laying down their Kalashnikovs as a young boy brought an enamel bowl of water, a pink Lux soap, and a grubby pink hand towel for us each to wash our hands. As the only woman, I was served last.

The boy then returned with a large aluminum dish of greasy goat stew swimming in globules of yellow fat and long slabs of stretchy Afghan bread to dip into it. All of it was washed down with curd in iced water, passed around in a shared cup. Wryly I remembered the British diplomat. As we ate the only sound was the appreciative smacking of lips. Silhouettes flickered on the mud walls in the light of the oil lamp.

"Eat well, as I don't know when we will get meat again," urged Karzai. He was right and I should have listened, but that night I was intent on avoiding the fat.

Over the next few weeks as we traveled to Kandahar, I got used to the fear of mines and helicopters, though everywhere we went we seemed to get bombed—perhaps connected to Karzai's habit of radioing everyone to say he'd arrived despite being on the Soviet hit list. Only when we had a narrow escape in the orchards of the Arghandab Valley did I get him to stop.

But I never got used to the lack of food. Occasionally we would be given shelter in a home in one of the mud-walled villages, which looked like something from biblical times, and villagers would share their meager supplies.

Our destination was a place called Malajat on the outskirts of Kandahar, run by a commander called Borjan. There we switched to Yamaha motorbikes, on which we could travel through the tall green cornfields without being detected. For about ten days we stayed in a small shack with a walled garden. At night I had my own room—actually, it was the ammo store with a curtain separating it from the main room, guarded by a young man called Abdul Wasei, who took his duties very seriously. Occasionally we even got a bucket of water to wash in. But there was nothing to eat except okra fried in kerosene and rock-hard naan and the ubiquitous green tea drunk with boiled sweets as there was no sugar.

Later, when I compared notes with other journalists, I realized how lucky I was I never got sick. I guess years of late-night meals from the Death Kebab van at university had given me a cast-iron stomach. But how I fantasized about the cheeseburgers and cold beer in the American Club!

There was not much to do. Once we went on a crazy late-night raid into the city to try to take out a Soviet guard post; our sortie failed dismally and ended with us running like crazy to try to get back. Mostly we just sat around. Sometimes the mujahideen picked flowers to put in their hair or tie to their guns. One day Ratmullah found a little sparrow, which he tied by a string to a multibarrel rocket launcher. Some of the fighters amused themselves by firing Kalashnikovs near it to make it jump.

Then one night Borjan told us we were going to attack the Kandahar air base where the Russians were stationed. Today it's the base of NATO operations for the south, referred to as K Town and complete with a boardwalk where you can find Pizza Hut, Tim Hortons coffee, and a TGI Friday's featuring surf-and-turf suppers and Elvis posters.

The plan was to depart at dawn, but we ended up leaving late morning. There were about twenty of us, all on motorbikes. I sat behind Ratmullah, trying to balance without touching his body so as not to offend him, and consequently almost falling off. My turban kept slipping down over my eyes and threatening to unravel.

But it felt good to be outside the shed—until we passed a tractor with the driver's body hanging off the side. His brains had been blown out.

We motored into a mulberry wood, where we stopped and hid the bikes in a branch-covered hole. Then we all passed under a Koran held by Ratmullah. Through the trees we ran and eventually down into one of trenches the mujahideen had built in rings around the city.

In the distance were some hills, and beyond that was the airport. Some men took up positions in the trench while others climbed into a tower, one of many used for drying grapes that are scattered around the south. From there they began firing rockets toward the airport, hoping to blow up a tank or fighter jet.

A shout went up and I saw Ratmullah's face crease with panic, then he pulled me down to the bottom of the trench. Two Soviet tanks had appeared on the crest of the hill and were rolling down toward us. It was an agony of waiting before they began firing, then there was a dull thud as the raisin tower behind us was hit, sending hot dust and rubble down on us.

Abdul Wasei dragged me into a foxhole in the side of the trench. We could hear the cries of the wounded, but there was nothing we could do. After a while the silence was almost worse.

And the tanks did not go away. All day they stayed there, leaving us stuck in our trenches, not daring to emerge.

We had nothing to eat or drink, and my tongue felt thick in my mouth. There were odd pools of muddy water in the trench, which the mujahideen scooped up in their hands and drank. The water was brown with mosquitoes feasting on top, and I couldn't imagine what diseases it might carry. But soon I was too thirsty to care. I too began scooping it into my hands and mouth. Mostly it tasted dusty.

Ratmullah suddenly jabbered excitedly in Pashto and held something up in his large hands. It was a mud crab. He bit into it, making noises of delight. Soon all the others were scratching the ground for mud crabs. Ratmullah offered one to me, but I shook my head. I wasn't sure how starved I would need to be to eat that.

Finally, on the second day, the tanks went away, presumably deciding we were all dead or gone. We ran along the trenches and eventually back out into the mulberry woods. As we emerged into the trees, the first thing I saw was a small boy eating watermelon, juice dripping from his mouth. I had never wanted anything so badly in my life. "Ratmullah, I want that watermelon," I said shamelessly.

Without hesitation Ratmullah grabbed it from the bewildered child. Nothing had ever tasted so good in my life.

When we got back to the hut, it felt like home. Everyone was talking excitedly. I turned the dial of my shortwave radio to BBC World Service, all static and crackle. Suddenly Louis Armstrong's "What a Wonderful World" came across the airwaves. It was a magical moment that afterward I thought I must have imagined. How would I have got that on the air in remote Afghanistan?

That night, our last in Kandahar, we had rice with a thin gruel crunchy with tiny bits of meat and bone. The next day as we left to head back to Pakistan, I realized that the sparrow had disappeared.

MUNTHER CANNOT COOK YOUR TURKEY

~IRAQ~

RAJIV CHANDRASEKARAN

BACK WHEN SADDAM HUSSEIN RULED IRAQ, MOST FOREIGN VISITORS were required to stay at the Hotel al-Rasheed, a concrete-and-glass monstrosity in central Baghdad. It was once a fine establishment, with marble floors and crystal chandeliers, but by the eve of George W. Bush's war the modern facade belied an intolerable interior. You had to bribe the housekeeper for a roll of toilet paper or a bar of soap. The televisions offered just three channels: Baathist agitprop, Iraqi sport, and bad 1970s movies dubbed into Arabic. The in-room surveillance cameras installed by the secret police had long since broken, but nobody knew that then, so female guests took to changing with the shower curtain drawn. But the biggest vexation was the daily breakfast scam. The buffet, served up in the Sheherazade Café, was atrocious: stale bread, cold omelets floating in grease, eggs boiled so long the yolks had turned gray, rotting fruit covered with flies. After two mornings of this horror, for which I had the pleasure of paying sixty thousand dinars a day—about thirty dollars at the exchange rate back then—I told the front desk I no longer wanted to eat breakfast, at least not in their restaurant.

"I'm sorry, sir, but we must charge you for the breakfast," the manager informed me.

"But I'm not eating your breakfast," I protested.

It did no good. "It is the rules," he said.

Then he leaned toward me and let me in on the secret. The fifty-dollar-a-night room charge went directly to Saddam's treasury. The only way for the hotel to pay its employees was by gouging us in the mornings. "Without breakfast," he said, sotto voce, "we cannot survive."

I tried to stomach the buffet, but after another two mornings I concluded that there was no way I'd survive in Baghdad with that breakfast. I raised the matter with Khalid, my enterprising driver, who kept a Shakira tape on continuous playback in his royal blue Chevy Caprice. He had boasted to me that he had an illegal satellite dish at home, and friends with an even more verboten Internet connection. Did he know of somewhere else I could eat breakfast?

In those days, food was hard to come by in Baghdad. Most families subsisted on government-issued rations of wheat, sugar, and rice. The few restaurants that catered to foreigners served only lunch and dinner. Khalid said he'd make some inquiries, but he made no promises.

A few days later, he beckoned me toward his car and said, "Mr. Rajiv, let's go for a drive." We headed west toward Mansur, the neighborhood filled with imposing mansions inhabited by Saddam's apparatchiks. He barreled down the main drag and pulled off near a small row of shops. Khalid pointed at one. The sign read Al-Malik Market. "Go in there," he said. "You will find what you need."

Malik was a culinary smuggler's dream. There was Heinz ketchup, Kellogg's corn flakes, Campbell's soup, and Ritz crackers. Seemingly everything you'd find in an American Safeway was packed into this little store—and several items even had Safeway price tags. I later learned that the owner's son traveled to Jordan once a week, where he filled up three taxis with a few of everything off the shelves at the Safeway in Amman. In twelve hours, after a couple of well-placed bribes to customs inspectors at the border, the food was for sale in Baghdad. Chilled, smoked Norwegian salmon? Yup.

Philly cream cheese and a bottle of capers? Sure. They had frozen pork bacon and tinned hams, which, in the predominantly Muslim Republic of Iraq, were about as forbidden as pornography. I even saw a Butterball turkey in the freezer. "*Aliseesh*," the owner said, teaching me the Arabic word for it. Who, I asked, buys turkeys in Baghdad? Nobody, he said. His son picked it up on spec, and it had been sitting in the cooler for a year.

Malik existed because, despite the UN sanctions that restricted oil sales, there still were thousands of Baathist cronies who had grown rich through smuggling and had dollars to blow. And unlike their neighbors, Iraqis of a certain age and class had traveled to Europe and America back in the 1960s and 1970s, before the wars with Iran and Kuwait, when one dinar was worth more than three dollars. They had a taste for Western food, for French cheese and Danish cookies. But like so much else in their country, these were luxuries out of reach to all but a few.

I shopped like a glutton. Wedges of Brie, fruit preserves, muesli, mango juice—more than I could fit in the mini-fridge back in my room, and more than I could consume before it would all spoil. Malik soon became my little escape from the chaos of prewar Baghdad. When I grew tired of Saddam's fulminations, the orchestrated protests we were obliged to attend, the UN weapons inspectors running from one installation to another, the maddening arguments with the Ministry of Information about their draconian rules, I headed back to the market, fished a few hundred-dollar bills out of my wallet, and filled up a basket with comfort food.

Soon after U.S. troops arrived in Baghdad, I headed back to Malik. I was in charge of the *Washington Post*'s bureau, and my responsibilities included ensuring that a half-dozen colleagues didn't go hungry. We had been subsisting on military rations and cans of beans and tuna fish that we had squirreled away before the invasion. Our supplies were running low, and I was yearning for slightly more gourmet provisions. But like so much else in Baghdad at the time, Malik had been gutted by looters. There were some broken jars on the floor, but everything else had been taken, even the freezer case and the turkey inside.

I despaired for a moment, and then it came to me: *I'll just do what the owner's son did.* I had a colleague visit a supermarket in Amman and fill up a GMC Suburban. The result, unfortunately, was more tuna and two cases of Cheez-Its. There was, thankfully, also a case of Pinot Grigio, and the realization that with a proper shopping list we could sustain ourselves without Malik.

Soon the need for shipments became less acute. The end of dictatorship meant we could move into a hotel with a decent kitchen, and then into a comfortable house a block from the Tigris River. I hired a chef named Munther, who scoured the markets for ingredients to indulge his experiments with Western cooking. One day we got a Waldorf salad. There was crème brûlée for dessert, albeit a little too sweet and runny. When a young reporter in the bureau came back with a Whopper and onion rings from the new Burger King at the military base next to the airport, Munther decided to copy the meal. The burgers, made from sheep that had been grazing on garbage, were a bit gamy, but the onion rings were perfect—crunchy, perfectly circular, and the size of half-dollars.

I put on fifteen pounds that first summer. Munther served up a three-course feast every night, donning a white jacket as he brought his creations into the dining room. I gave him carte blanche to buy whatever he wanted— figuring that with Malik closed, he couldn't get into too much trouble— and he managed to find a seemingly endless variety of produce. The lack of supermarkets meant everything was made from scratch. He baked the bread and trimmed the meat and simmered the sauces.

In idle moments, over cups of tea and cigarettes, I came to learn about the lives of the Iraqis who worked for us as interpreters, drivers, and guards. One had been a pilot for Iraqi Airways. Another was a mechanical engineer who had a master's degree from UCLA. And yet another had worked as a

driver for the general security directorate before the war, no doubt shuttling people to torture sessions. But Munther remained a mystery. He
spoke little English, so every conversation required an intermediary. Every
interaction was transactional: What do you want for dinner tomorrow? Can
I buy a new meat grinder? My efforts to engage always seemed to fall flat.
After a few months, all I knew about him was that he was in his thirties. He
was lanky and had close-cropped hair. He arrived in the afternoons with a
stack of Arabic books and kept to himself in the kitchen. He left as we tucked
into dessert. Where did he learn to cook? How did he feel about making
sumptuous meals for a bunch of Americans while millions of Iraqis were
still living hand to mouth? I had no idea.

One day I walked into the kitchen as he entered from the back door. He
placed his books in two stacks, and I pointed to them with a quizzical expression. He gestured to one pile. "Shia books," he said. Then the other. "Cookbooks." I beckoned an interpreter to join us, but we were able to wrest only
the most meager details about his life. He had grown up in the overwhelm-
ingly Shiite south, and by the time he was in his late teens, he was torn between his desire to train as a cook and his desire to rebel at the oppression of
his fellow Shiites by Saddam's regime. His religious activism soon landed
him in prison, where he was tortured so brutally that he lost hearing in one
ear. When he was finally released, a few years before the war, he managed to
land a job as an apprentice in a Baghdad restaurant. When the restaurant
closed after the invasion, the owner sent him my way.

That's all I got. Despite the white jacket and Waldorf salads, I could tell
he was ambivalent about working for a bunch of foreigners. Sure, the
money was good, and he got to experiment in ways he never could in a kebab restaurant, but he was cooking in a house where the occupants drank
wine and the women let their hair flow freely. Of the three dozen Iraqis
who worked for me, he was the most conflicted. At the time, I thought him
an anomaly. I blithely assumed most Iraqis were like the rest of my staff—

guys who liked to sneak a beer and check out pornographic sites on the office computers; one young interpreter was so enamored of the United States that he took to wearing an American flag T-shirt. Munther never socialized with them. He holed up in the kitchen.

In the following months, I tried to win him over. When I was in California for a holiday, I bought him a ten-inch Wüsthof chef's knife and a cookbook with photos so he could pick out recipes he wanted translated. Our vegetables were chopped a little finer, and the menu became more varied, but he didn't become any less standoffish.

In mid-December, U.S. forces found Saddam hiding in a hole, and any hopes I had of spending Christmas with my family in California were shot as quickly as the celebratory gunfire that lit up the Baghdad sky. I decided to host a secular Christmas Eve dinner at our house. It would be a chance to see friends in Baghdad with whom I had lost touch because of hectic work schedules. It would be a way to expose our Iraqi colleagues to new traditions. And it would give me a chance to challenge Munther with his most complicated meal yet.

The essential ingredient, of course, was an *aliseesh*. But with Malik still closed and my supply convoys from Jordan suspended because of banditry on the highway from Jordan, I had to find a new smuggler. I approached a few shopkeepers, but none of them was willing to try. Then, on the advice of a friend, I went to a market in the city's Christian quarter that was so secretive it had no sign or door from the street. To get in, I had to go through an unlit adjoining building. When I entered, I discovered why: there were cases of whiskey, gin, and beer amid a Maliklike assortment of foreign foodstuffs. I inquired about a turkey. "Come back in three days," the man said. I thought about asking whether it would come from Jordan and, if so, whether it would be kept cold. Or would it be packed into the hot trunk of a taxi with a dozen boxes of Cheerios? Or did he have a connection on a military base who'd slip him a bird under the barbed wire? I kept silent and purchased a bottle of whiskey.

When I returned home, I asked Munther whether he had ever cooked an *aliseesh*. Never, he said. Did any of his books have instructions for how to prepare one? Not that he had seen. Since these were the days before one sought answers to every random question on Google, I did what I always do when I find myself in a culinary fix: I called my mother—on a costly satellite phone—and asked her to e-mail me her turkey recipe.

On December 23, we got word from the market: *Come get your turkey.* There, in a waist-high chest freezer, was a genuine Butterball turkey. Fifteen pounds. Frozen as a rock.

Munther showed up early the next morning to prepare the feast, which would also include roast beef, potatoes au gratin, sautéed peas and carrots, fried zucchini, rice, and a *fattoush* salad. I printed out my mother's turkey recipe, gave it to one of my Iraqi colleagues to translate for Munther, and then settled down to write a story.

An hour later, there was a knock on my room door. I opened it to find one of my interpreters and a grave-faced Munther.

"Munther cannot cook your turkey," the interpreter said.

"Why not?"

"The recipe calls for wine," the interpreter said. "He cannot touch any alcohol."

"It's just for the broth and to baste the turkey," I said. "All the alcohol will evaporate in the heat of the oven and the stove." But Munther was adamant. He wasn't going to touch the turkey or the broth. "Fine," I huffed, "I'll do it myself." And I walked down to the kitchen, uncorked a bottle of Chablis, and set about preparing the turkey.

As I was assembling the ingredients for the broth, Munther came up to me with the interpreter. He cracked a smile. He noted that I had thrown a large party for the Iraqi staff and their families a month earlier to celebrate the Eid al-Fitr holiday after the monthlong Ramadan fast. Because of that, and because the recipe was from my mother, and because I promised him that the alcohol would evaporate, he said he would cook the turkey. "You respected our traditions, so I will respect yours," he said. And with that, he shooed me out of the kitchen.

It was the sort of grudging, uneasy accommodation that came to define the American presence in Iraq. The rest of the staff were like the exiles who sought power in the early days: unabashedly pro-Western and modern, eager to please and happy to change. But Munther was the real Iraq: strong, proud, conservative, tradition-bound, and more than a little bit stubborn. There was common ground to be had, but it wasn't going to be achieved easily.

I hate oven-roasted turkey. Thanksgiving is my least favorite meal of the year. At Christmas, I always lobbied my mother to make fish or lasagna or even Indian food. Why I sought out a turkey in Baghdad that year is beyond me. Perhaps I was going a bit mad after all those months in a war zone. Perhaps I just wanted a Butterball because it seemed so crazy and unattainable. Whatever the motivation, Munther's turkey looked as perfect as the fake one Bush carried when he visited the troops on Thanksgiving. Golden brown. Crispy wings. Juices oozing down the sides.

He put it on a silver platter and placed it on the table, next to the potatoes and rice and all the trimmings. Munther was beaming as we walked in from the living room.

"Merry Christmas," he said. And then he began slicing the turkey.

It was, everyone agreed, the best meal they had eaten in Baghdad. When we finished, I walked into the kitchen to thank Munther, but as usual, he had departed as soon as we began dessert.

"Did Munther eat before he left?" I asked the young man washing dishes.

He did, I was told. He ate the roast beef and the potatoes and the rice. He ate everything, the young man said, except the turkey.

This is the e-mail from my mother containing the recipes, reproduced verbatim:

Rajiv,

The turkey should be thawed. If yours is still frozen, immerse it in water, keep changing the water as it thaws. If all else fails—extreme measures—your cook can hack it in half (saw or machete?) and then cook it!!! Do not use a kitchen knife to cut a frozen turkey.

Assuming that you have a thawed bird:
Other ingredients: Few cloves of garlic, 2 onions, 5–6 carrots, few ribs of celery, parsley, herbs, butter, salt, and pepper
Remove the neck and the giblets. If you have a frozen turkey from the States, then check both the abdominal cavity as well the neck cavity for plastic bags with the neck and giblets. Save the neck for broth. I do not like the taste of the giblets so I throw them out.

Broth: Put the neck (and giblets if you wish) in a saucepan, cover with water, add half of the vegetables—chopped carrots, onions, celery (if you have any) garlic, parsley and some herbs (e.g., oregano, marjoram or poultry spices, if you have some, salt, pepper). Bring to a boil and simmer for a couple of hours. I also add some white wine to this while it is simmering . . . about a cup. Strain and reserve the broth.

Turkey without stuffing: This cooks faster and is safer.
Rinse the turkey and dry both inside and out. Place the remaining vegetables (above) with an apple cut into quarters plus some salt and pepper in the abdominal cavity.

Rub the outside of bird with some soft butter. I also put some butter and herbs between the skin and the breast meat. You will have to do it carefully so that you do not tear the skin. Truss the bird . . . that is, close the abdominal cavity with skewers and tie the legs with a piece of string.

Preheat the oven to 425 degrees.

Place the turkey in a roasting pan on a rack. I add more of the above chopped vegetables and herbs with more garlic and parsley. Add a cup of water and some wine to the pan. Place in oven.

After 20 minutes reduce heat to 325 degrees.

Bake approx. 15–20 minutes per pound. If you have a thermometer the breast meat should register 165 and the thigh 180. If not, the old method was to jiggle the leg and pierce the thigh. The juices should not be pink.

If the breast (which usually cooks faster) browns too quickly, cover (tent) the turkey loosely with some foil.

When the bird is done, remove from oven and let it rest about 25–30 minutes before carving.

Gravy: Discard vegetables (press out the juices with a spoon) and excess fat from the roasting pan. Strain and save the drippings. In a heavy saucepan melt 3 tablespoons butter and add 3 tablespoons flour and cook till golden. Watch carefully so that it does not burn. Take off the stove and gradually add the broth (2 cups) and the drippings, blending constantly with a whisk. You can also add few tablespoons of sherry, port or Madeira. Cook over medium heat till it thickens. Stir constantly while cooking. Add salt and pepper.

Potato Gratin: Serves about 6–8 people. Increase quantity for larger group.
3 lbs potatoes, peeled and sliced in quarters
4 garlic cloves, minced
4 tablespoons finely chopped parsley
1 cup shredded cheese (usually gruyere). Use what you have . . . parmesan?
Pepper and salt
1 cup of broth (from the turkey recipe if you have extra) or some half and half—mix cream and some milk
Butter

In a greased baking dish place a layer of potatoes. Sprinkle garlic, cheese, parsley, and seasonings. Continue layers ending with garlic, cheese, etc. on top. Pour broth or cream on top. Dot with butter. Bake for an hour till the potatoes are tender. Top should be golden.

Good luck! Call me if you need any clarification.
Mom

P.S. If you need any other recipes, email me with a list of items available and I will send something.

~PART FOUR~
BREAKING BREAD

THE BEST MAN I EVER KNEW

~GEORGIA~

WENDELL STEAVENSON

I GOT IT INTO MY HEAD ONCE TO FIGURE OUT WHAT HAD STARTED THE Abkhazian war. It was 1999 and I was living in Tbilisi, the capital of the post-Soviet Republic of Georgia in the southern Caucasus. It was five years since the Abkhas (with some meddling help from the Russians) had defeated the Georgian army and pushed a quarter of a million ethnic Georgians out of their homes along the pebbly Black Sea coast. The displaced families still filled every grand hotel in Tbilisi, strung up their washing on the mini-balconies, punched holes in the walls for tin-can chimney pipes. The refugees were making do with patched-up remnants, but all of Georgia was essentially camping in a shell of its former self during those limbo years. The country was in stasis: flatline economy, electricity down to four hours a day. The streets chugged with generators, a fug of kerosene hugged my apartment. Luckily I had a stove fueled by a gas canister, but I cooked by candlelight, peering into obscure saucepans and dripping wax on the potatoes.

Half British, half American, I had grown up safe in the assumption of historical progress. I had absorbed the Whig theory of liberal democratic determinism and the American belief in economic growth and the deliverance of technology. But I was living in Georgia, in the husk of the Soviet

Empire, where time had run backward and now hung about listlessly. The tropes of civilization, the normal about-your-business quotidian of life— police, courts, state salaries and pensions, municipal heat—had all but stopped. The long corridors of power were dark, their parquet warped and the offices on either side only intermittently occupied by officials who found it convenient to conduct their business from a government phone line. I began to grimace at the palliative idioms I had formerly parroted and which now stuck in my throat, trite and false: "darkest before the dawn," "tomorrow's another day," "things can only get better."

"It's all a bullshit! Pah!" Zaliko would shake his head and pour another glass of homemade wine from a plastic five-liter jerican. In Georgia this comment was universally applicable. I would stick my feet in the fire to warm them and listen to his funny, scurrilous stories of self-serving parliamentarians and businessmen-bandit-thugs and dinosaur apparatchiks who still loomed in the shadows. Zaliko was an archaeologist by training, a mountaineer by passion, and a humanitarian by default; he believed in no ideology or institution except that of human kindness, and he was the best man I ever knew.

Zaliko was in his fifties when I first met him and he invited me to tea in the railroad apartment, housed under the sloping tin roof of a collapsing pre-Revolutionary house on a hidden lane off a cobbled street in the center of Tbilisi, that his family had occupied for a couple of generations. His two children were young adults, grown and married, and he lived with his widowed father; his wife, the beautiful and long-suffering (for anything Zaliko had, he immediately gave away) Marina, who worked for the Soros Foundation; and his younger, soft-spoken brother Zura, a puppeteer, who had never married but whom all children instinctively loved. The family had survived the civil war years that coincided with the ethnic wars in Abkhazia and South Ossetia (another ethnic oblast engineered by a Stalinist pen stroke across a map) by making cheese from the milk of two cows they kept at their ramshackle dacha up a picturesque ravine a little way out of the city.

"Don't laugh at cheese!" Sometimes Zaliko's long nose and long gray beard appeared to give him an admonishing clerical expression, but then his deep-set currant eyes would twinkle with an impish sense of the ridiculous and any notion of reprimand was dispelled. "Two years we lived in cheese!" He laughed with great seriousness. Zura staged a full-length puppet satire spectacular about a group of Georgian cows who longed for lush Swiss pastures. One of my favorite scenes was a re-creation of a grandiloquent communist May Day Parade, complete with banging drums and triumphant trumpets, when all the cows proudly marched under banners proclaiming, "Cheese Is Freedom!"

Zaliko and I sat several winters by his fire, tracing histories and stories on the old faded and worn map of Georgia that covered an entire wall. Often there were visitors: an old friend, now broken down and wearing a threadbare overcoat; a visiting American professor of ethnography who had brought him a fresh supply of *National Geographic* magazines; a pair of young climbers embarking on an expedition to Everest; Chechen refugees from the Pankisi Gorge hoping to set up a computer center. One Chechen I remember, nervous and scratchy, hollowed out with heroin and begging more money when the computers were all, inevitably, stolen. We would sit around the table covered in papers and books and Zaliko would buzz in and out of the kitchen, making tea, pouring wine, bringing out a bowlful of *jonjolia,* a tangle of pickled white flowers, or a hunk of aged salty ammoniac cheese. Sometimes he fried up *kupati,* chicken-guts sausage, thick and black, coiled and oil-rich like the innards of a disassembled engine. In the summer he would take me up to the dacha and build a fire with dried vine cuttings, which he said made the best heat, and roast skewers of pork for *mtsvadi,* tossing the crackling meat with ruby pomegranate seeds.

We sat by the fire and I learned my Georgian history. It was a litany of defeat: Romans, Greeks, Tamerlane, Persians, Ottomans, Russians. . . .

"But the Georgians are even better at fighting among themselves!" Zaliko snorted half in derision, half with a certain rueful, stubborn pride. He told me stories that crisscrossed the waves of invasion with countercurrents of long-lost feudal alliances, traitor princes, highlander defiance, fortress monasteries, kidnappings, massacres, hostage sons. All along the roads we drove in his secondhand Soviet army jeep, among the stripped-for-scrap abandoned ruins of Soviet factories, he pointed out the tumulus remains of razed villages and the fragments of crenellated walls that still clung to steep promontories.

Once during the civil war—it must have been about 1991, when there was fighting around the Parliament building—Zaliko was on duty with the Red Cross. Sheltering in a doorway in a side street he had caught sight of his father, head up, stride unchecked by zinging bullets, a small shopping bag looped around one wrist, on his way to buy some eggs and cigarettes.

"Go home, old man!" Zaliko shouted across the street between scatter-shot fusillades. "It's dangerous! There's fighting here!"

"Pah!" shouted back his father, who had been to Berlin with the Red Army. "This is not fighting. This is just boys!"

When the war in Abkhazia began, Zaliko's son, Archil, was seventeen and got himself fired up with all the pride-of-small-nations bravado and nationalist flag-waving. He wanted to go off and fight for his country. Zaliko had to forcibly stop him.

"Pah!" he told him, "do you think you will be a man if you play with these boys?"

Empires had come and conquered, but somehow the Georgians remained. They had kept their polyphonic harmonies and their hexagonal churches and their language with its macaroni curlicued alphabet. I began to suspect that the Georgians knew they could never win on the battlefield and had learned a subtler tactic for survival, lulling the invader into leniency with excess hospitality. The Roman legionnaire, the Persian satrap, the Ottoman general, the Russian engineer would find himself in front of a table overladen with dozens of dishes: pounded spinach with walnuts and marigold spice, lamb stew with sour green plums and tarragon, cold roast suckling pig with purple plum sauce, hot, crumbly rounds of *khachapuri* cheese bread, a stew of tomatoes and aubergines, stuffed mushrooms, pickled garlic, minced pork kebabs, crispy fried corn bread, milky *sulguni* cheese. The *tamada,* or toastmaster, would raise his wine horn and drink to mothers and to the motherland, to old friends we have lost, and new friends we have just made, to the sacred grape (Georgia is the oldest center of viticulture in the world), king and emperor, to ancestors and grandchildren yet to come—and foreigners would find themselves charmed and beguiled, quite drunk and the object of such lavish affection that they could not stop grinning. The *supra* became Georgia's most enduring national pastime. Any excuse: arrival, departure, birthday, funeral. In the nineteenth century, sixty-seven separate *religious* feast days were identified.

"No wonder Georgia never got around to industrializing," I teased Zaliko. Georgians shrugged at their lackadaisical obstinacy; they had no need for modern invention and intervention. During Soviet times, visiting delegations from Siberian industrial combines were invariably treated—subjected to the ploy of the generous *supra*-fest. It was an effective strategy, even in the land of the production committee. Georgian businessmen managed to insert themselves into every nook and cranny amid the cogs of the great inefficient mechanism of the command economy. Georgia sent its wine and famous salty Borjomi mineral water, its mandarins and hazelnuts north, and in return received cars and fridges. In 1989, when everything went to hell, Georgians had the highest savings per capita of any republic in the Soviet Union.

Despite the cushy arrangement, the thwarted pride of a nationalist heart beat in every Georgian chest. Perhaps the Abkhazian war was the result of the Georgians becoming momentarily overexcited, finding themselves in the unusual position of the biggest kid on the playground instead of the littlest. Perhaps the Russians fanned the flames of mistrust between Georgians and

Abkhas because a war allowed their machinating intervention. Perhaps it was easy enough just to say, "it's the Caucasus"—tribe, honor, feud—and shrug.

"You want to know what started the Abkhaz war?" Zaliko asked, spooning out a little honey from a giant amber jar he had been given by an old friend with a hive near Zugdidi ("Did you know they preserve bodies in honey in Mingrelia?"). "Ask Jaba!"

Jaba had been the most prominent of the warlords during the years of civil and ethnic war. In 1999 he had recently been released from prison, and he was still vain enough to agree to talk. In the yard of his apartment block I came across his eight-year-old grandson, also called Jaba, playing ambush in the courtyard with a plastic Kalashnikov. Little Jaba nodded at me gravely, as if vetting my entry. The door was opened by Jaba's wife and I was ushered into the parlor, where a table was set for tea: a pink-and-roses tea set with gold trim, a saucer of lemon slices, a small bowl of peaches in syrup, and a plate of sliced cake: a dense coffee sponge soaked in brandy and covered in swirls of chocolate whipped cream with a cherry on top. This faux-opulent cake tasted like mealy wet cardboard with chemical cream; it reminded me of the rococo gilded-veneer pastiches of French eighteenth-century furniture that the Soviets had copied from Romanov palaces and were to be found, invariably, in the grande-luxe corners of former apparatchiks' apartments.

Jaba, tall, unbowed, with short-cut steel-colored hair, smiled sharkishly at my questions. I asked him about August 14, 1992, the day hostilities had begun, when a group of Georgian soldiers had opened fire in a small seaside town on the Abkhazian coast. On whom exactly was unclear. Why? and On whose orders? were other unanswered questions. I had begun to think of this incident as the fulcrum moment, a volley of violence that tipped everything suddenly into war. With hindsight it looked inevitable—tensions between Georgians and Abkhas had been seething for months—but *inevitable* is a word that can be used only in hindsight.

Jaba told me that he had been in Kutaisi on the day in question and nowhere near the events in Abkhazia. He refused to specify further. It was a complicated time—he waved his hands in circles—Shevardnadze had just come back but was not yet elected, there were no phone lines, no one knew what was going on, the Georgian National Guard was all split up under different commands, Gamsakhurdia's supporters had kidnapped ministers. . . .

"You should ask Kitovani these things," he said, referring me to the second most powerful warlord of that era, and then smiled as he held up a delicate filigreed china plate. "Some more cake?"

The Georgian defense of Sokhumi, the capital of Abkhazia, collapsed in October 1994. The Georgians who fled from their homes along the subtropical littoral were still wearing their summer clothes, but in the mountains there was already snow on the ground. Zaliko went with his old mountain rescue friends to help the refugees through the high passes. He carried an old sick man on his back for several hours. Mothers juggled toddlers; grandmothers pushed handcarts; soldiers stumbled, wounded, exhausted, carrying their comrades on stretchers. The forest verges and clearings were full of the detritus of flight: abandoned heavy vinyl suitcases, scraps of muddy clothing, a loose goat, the dazed, the dying.

Zaliko and others tried to get the old and sick onto helicopters, but there were not many helicopters, the ground was jagged and high, the weather froze and rolled mist, and it was hard to land. One pilot couldn't bear to turn desperate people away, and a huge crowd crammed into his hold. Zaliko watched as the helicopter lifted off the ground and swayed toward the ridge ahead, then rolled inexorably like a great hippo, crashing into the mountainside. He and his colleagues climbed up to the burning mass of metal and people to try to help any survivors. Zaliko spent the night with a woman dying of her injuries.

Kitovani had been released from prison two years earlier. I talked to him in the back of his black Mercedes, with a bodyguard in the front seat. He was squat and fleshy like a toad, kept his sunglasses on throughout the interview, and said nothing of any interest that did not serve his own.

Zaliko often visited some families he knew among the refugees from Abkhazia, brought them lengths of pink sausage or a plastic Coke bottle or two filled with his homemade firewater, *chacha*. He seemed to be a one-man NGO, a freelance humanitarian. He was one of the very few Georgians at that time who used to go up to South Ossetia, and he maintained a rare point of informal contact with moderate Ossetians, despite plenty of his acquaintances muttering "traitor" under their breath. He drove me up to Tskhinvali, the capital (scarcely an hour and a half from Tbilisi), on a raw wintry day, through the black market that sold cheap Russian goods—almost exclusively lurid yellow soda and gasoline of the same color—on the unrecognized border. We were met by two young men, earnest enough and friendly and glad to have some help with some project or another, but I remember them looking over their shoulders in case someone saw them fraternizing with the enemy.

My efforts—I talked to historians, ex-soldiers, politicians, journalists—to identify the moment, the order, the misunderstanding, the spark that had caused those Georgian soldiers to open fire on August 14, came to naught. Nobody knew or especially, it seemed, wanted to. I harbored a dreadful suspicion that there was no particular reason or order for the shooting at all. It need not have happened, it had been a random mistake, a spur-of-the-moment reaction.

The following summer my brother came to visit me in Georgia, and Zaliko took us up into the mountains, rattling up the stone road to the northern slopes of the Caucasus, to the vertiginous meadow sweeps of Khevsureti. We walked up high over piebald snow slopes, through freezing snowmelt rivers in bare feet to keep our shoes dry, past slate shrines surmounted with goat skulls, and into the valley of Arkhoti for a ceremonial horse race.

In the mountains Zaliko was half goat, wiry, strong, and lithe, half mischievous Pan, striding up a near-vertical track with a cheap Viceroy cigarette hanging out of the side of his mouth and a hundred pounds of clinking bottles (*chacha* and plum sauce accounted for the bulk of his baggage) on his back. When we stopped to rest I would bend over my knees to steady the lightheaded space of veering height against my jelly knees, and Zaliko would reach inside his shirt pocket and produce a magical plastic bag of lemon slices and sugar that had been macerated into a bright delicious sludge by the action of his stride.

"Very good for energy!"

Khevsurs, rosy-cheeked highlanders, came from surrounding valleys and villages, tied their horses to a fence, and stacked their Kalashnikovs by the doors of the few houses. On the day of the race we feasted on boiled ox and tiny fried river fish and salads of finely diced radish, potato, and dill. The village elders drank ceremonial beer made from precious barley, and everyone else drank *chacha* till there was singing and fistfights, and the children ran around in loops catching skittish horses. That night Zaliko slept with his body across the entrance to my tent to protect me from kidnappers.

In other trips to the northern side of the Caucasus, Zaliko would tell me about village feuds and plague huts and describe the ingenious irrigation systems for abandoned slate villages or the asymmetrical plow that the uplanders used to cultivate such steep slopes. He often took supplies for the few poor families who stayed in Upper Khevsureti through the winter, cut off when the first snows blocked the passes. He passed out sixty-pound sacks of flour, quantities of macaroni and sugar, bags of peaches we had brought from the lowland farmers along the road, and, for the kids to share, a giant red watermelon or two.

We were camping in a meadow a few miles from the Chechen border one night when a lone man with a scraggly beard, wearing a camouflage jacket and a Kalashnikov across his back, emerged from the gloaming. I felt a sense of foreboding but Zaliko welcomed him warmly, tore off a chunk of bread and offered it to him, shared our supper, and poured our guest glass after glass of *chacha*. I sat watchful and quiet as Zaliko enthusiastically toasted the mountains, family, friendship, brotherhood, honor. The lone man drank tumbler after tumbler, and his suspicious stony expression softened in the firelight glow as the stars came out, livid above. When we packed up the next morning our visitor was still lying where he had collapsed, dead to the world, with his head on a rock for a pillow. Zaliko, strangely, was as sprightly as ever.

"Aha!" he tapped the side of his nose, "after the first two toasts, I am filling my glass with water!"

We drove out of the mountains, filthy, unslept, tired, and aching from the jolting stone flint roads. We stopped at Zaliko's favorite shack for *khinkali*—great fat dumplings of dough pleated into a topknot and filled with a nugget of ground pork surrounded by broth. You had to eat *khinkali* very carefully, balancing the scalding-hot rim of the dumpling against the forked topknot and biting gently to suck without losing any of the precious juice. I could manage only four or five, but Zaliko always ordered twenty because somehow it was a shame to order a paltry plate.

"Do you know the story of the man who ordered ninety-nine *khinkali*?" Zaliko's moustache twitched merrily. I shook my head. "The waitress asked him, 'Why not just order 100?' 'Oh, no!' said the man, patting his big round stomach proudly, 'I know my limits!'"

"He would give everything to everyone else!" Zaliko's wife, Marina, smiled, rueful, remembering his stubbornness. I had left Georgia in 2001 and had returned only intermittently, following the Rose Revolution from afar and keeping in touch with my friends. I marveled with them at the novelty of uncorrupt police, the new buildings going up, ATM machines, and home loans; everyone seemed a little more prosperous, Saakashvili's presidency had brought a buzz. Now it was the end of August 2008 as Marina and I reminisced. The Russians had pulled their tanks back to the South Osse-

tian border a few days before. I had spent the day in hospital wards, interviewing wounded soldiers and trying to piece together the events of another sudden war in the Caucasus, and Marina had just come back from
delivering food to refugee families.

We shared accounts. Marina made me a cup of tea and poured a little
wine Zura had made from the vines at the dacha. She put out a plate of hazelnuts, and as she talked she cracked them with a little hammer and placed
the naked kernels in a row for me to eat. I told her that the soldiers' wounds—
shrapnel, blasts, amputated limbs—were all from aerial bombardment.

"No small arms. Not a single bullet hole. They were smashed up by Russian air superiority. *Aviatsia.*" I used the Russian word. "They were brave, I
think—hiding, scattering, trying to regroup under the bombs—but their
orders were contradictory, no helicopters, radios were down—"

"Many of the refugees from the Georgian villages in South Ossetia are
in ZAKVO," Marina told me. I nodded; I had been to talk to families there
too. She said she had been making *lobio,* bean stew, and taking it to them in
the evenings. "What can we do? We can do something, but it is very small."
She shrugged wearily and smiled, beautiful as always, undimmed, almost
beatific.

ZAKVO was a giant hulk of 1970s architecture that had housed, in former
times, the headquarters for the southern Military Strategic Planning Authority of the Soviet Union. This was where Soviet generals had putatively planned
an invasion of NATO-allied Turkey. The Russians had only actually vacated
the building a few months before; in recent years it was rumored to have been
a leftover listening post. Marina and I rolled our eyes at the doomed-to-repeat
looping irony of the situation: Georgian refugees from a war promulgated,
encouraged, and egged on by Russia were now camping in the deserted offices once populated by Russian military officials planning wars.

Our conversation halted at some point, in deference to the sadness and
the weight of it.

"I'm so sorry I did not come for the funeral," I said, tears beginning to well along with chagrin at the too-many years that had passed before my return to Georgia. Marina shook her head.

"No, no. It was very far for you. And there were many, many people—all of Tbilisi it seemed came—"

Zaliko had died in 2005. He was killed in a climbing accident on Ushba, the treacherous mountain that rises, sheer, icy, and double-peaked, above Svaneti, the highest region in Georgia. Zaliko and two other Georgian mountaineers were guiding two Dutchmen to the summit when there was an accident of some kind. Mamuka, Zaliko's friend, was injured, equipment was lost, and the weather closed in. The third Georgian and the two Dutchmen continued up and climbed above the clouds, calling from mobile phones for a rescue party, but for several days Zaliko and Mamuka were missing. When the rescue party found Zaliko's frozen body, they said there was still a smile on his face. He had died in the mountains that he loved; he had died because he would not leave his dying friend.

"Everything he gave away," repeated Marina. I allowed a wan, inward smile; after all, she had just returned from feeding the hungry. "Especially his time. All his time and energy went on other people. And the last time we spoke I was angry with him and shouting down the telephone, because he did not even tell me he was in Svaneti. And when I heard where he was I was angry, because I had some premonition that he would try to climb Ushba."

A couple of days after I met Marina for coffee that afternoon, I got a commission to write a profile of President Saakashvili for an American magazine. I reported for more than a month, trying to disentangle the Georgian official version of the summer's events. I interviewed Saakashvili and his security team several times. Who shot first? Whose rockets were fired from which position? The tale was clogged with intercepted radio transmissions, public pronouncements, and Russian propaganda. The Georgians distorted sections of the timeline and tried to overwrite events with an official narrative. They clung to nationalist outrage and pointed north shouting, "The Russians! The Russians!" at the top of their lungs.

At 7:00 P.M. on August 7, as tensions and gunfire between South Ossetian militias and Georgian army and police posts was intensifying, Saakashvili had gone on television to declare a unilateral ceasefire. By midnight he was shelling the South Ossetian capital and had ordered a full-scale attack. What happened—or what he thought or guessed or hoped was happening—between those two decisions, I never discovered. The Georgian attack foundered, the Russians sent in armored columns. And in the middle of the worst of it, when the Russian tanks were rolling down the highway toward Tbilisi and the Americans continued to dither, Saakashvili was caught on a BBC satellite feed, as he waited to make another impassioned, desperate plea for Georgian democracy, munching the end of his tie like a demented man.

Another scrappy, brutal, stupid Caucasian war, meaningless and tragic. I missed Zaliko. I missed him telling me it was all "a bullshit."

DINNER WITH A JESTER
~AFGHANISTAN~

JON LEE ANDERSON

IN MARCH 2005, AN AFGHAN FRIEND INVITED ME TO JOIN HIM FOR dinner at the home of a relative who lived in the countryside near the market town of Charikar, some fifty miles north of Kabul. We would have to stay overnight, he said, because it was not safe to drive back after dark. Highwaymen were known to attack and rob motorists who ventured on the road at night. With the twinkly look of someone withholding a secret, he promised me that the evening would be a "special" one. Intrigued, I agreed to go along.

We drove for an hour northward across the fertile Shamali Plain that leads to Charikar, which sits where the foothills of the Hindu Kush begin. Beyond Charikar, the road begins to climb and wind and soon enters the narrow mouth of the fabled Panjshir Valley, which became a symbol of mujahideen resistance during the Soviet military occupation of Afghanistan. During their decade-long presence in the country, the Soviets proved unable to take the Panjshir. As testament to their failure, the roadsides of the valley are littered with the rusting hulks of their mangled tanks and armored personnel carriers. After they seized Kabul, Taliban fighters had massacred their way north across the Shamali Plain, but had been unable to take the Panjshir either. Their final frontline defenses with the Northern

Alliance had been fixed just south of Charikar until they abandoned them and melted away in November 2001, following six weeks of sustained American aerial bombardment.

Since the Taliban rout, hundreds of the Shamali's war-displaced farmers had returned to their shattered lands and begun to rebuild and replant, even as the UN's mine-clearance experts worked to clear the fields and roads around them. Beyond the old front line around Charikar, however, the orchards and vineyards were abundant with fruit, and the irrigation canals sparkled with fresh snowmelt.

We eventually came to a mud-walled compound. There we were greeted by our host, Atta, a thin man in his late thirties. My friend explained that Atta was his cousin and, effectively, a local warlord. He had been a commander for the Northern Alliance for many years, and was now a landowning farmer of some substance. Because of his past military status and his relative wealth, he remained the de facto authority in the area. Although it was no longer legal to do so, Atta kept fifty or so gunmen on his payroll. With the central government still weak, they helped enforce security in the area. If more fighters were ever needed, my friend explained, Atta could quickly summon additional volunteers from among his tenant farmers and his neighbors.

Atta waved us graciously into a long carpeted room strewn with pillows, where he introduced several shy-looking teenage boys as his younger brothers and nephews. A strongly built, dark-skinned older man stepped forward. My friend whispered excitedly that his name was Samad Pashean, and he was a traditional *maskhara*, or jester, of some renown. He had been invited to Atta's home at his request, and in my honor, to provide the evening's entertainment. Pashean shook my hand and held it in a firm grip as he stared boldly into my eyes. He had a mischievous face. My friend said, "I told you it would be a special evening." He smiled proudly.

This was indeed a rare treat. I had thought Afghanistan's *maskhara* to be an extinct species. For centuries, *maskhara* had entertained the country's monarchs with their japes and buffoonery, and by lampooning them. They may well have been the originators of the European tradition of court fools, as well, for *maskhara* is a term of Arabic or possibly Sanskrit origin, and along with the first royal jesters, words using the same root appeared in medieval Europe sometime in the thirteenth century, ultimately seeding the English language with such exoticisms as *mascara* and *mask*.

Samad Pashean, who estimated his age at sixty, was evidently one of Afghanistan's last remaining *maskhara*. He had survived the abolition of the monarchy, the Soviet military occupation, the ensuing bloody civil war, and then the Taliban years by wandering from one warlord's lair to another, plying his prankish wares in exchange for food, shelter, and the occasional handout of money. As my friend explained it, Atta had placed Pashean under his protection, maintaining him in a house nearby and giving him regular allotments of food from his harvests. Atta bade us all sit down as boys brought in large round trays heaped with salad, pilau rice, bowls of yogurt, mutton soup, fruit, baked chicken, and lamb, and laid them on the carpet in front of us.

Over our food, which we dug into with our hands, Atta boasted proudly of Pashean's many talents, telling me that in addition to his prowess as an entertainer, he was also a professional blackmailer, a master thief, and a prolific murderer, with an estimated fifty victims killed by his own hand. As Atta related this last statistic in delighted exclamation, the other men and boys in the room laughed and stared reverentially at Pashean, who grinned and nodded his head in acknowledgment.

After the trays with our food were taken away and we were sipping at sugary black tea and munching dried mulberries, Pashean began to perform, regaling us with vaudevillian skits and dances, bawdy jokes, and gossipy, extemporaneous riffs on everything from sex to politics. To the ecstatic amusement of Atta and his boys, Pashean acted out a skit that he called "The Unwilling Bride on Her Wedding Night." After encouraging one of the boys to play the "eager bridegroom," Pashean placed a turban cloth over his head to resemble a burka. As the "groom" got into the spirit of things by attempting to paw Pashean, giggling hysterically as he did so, Pashean was transformed into a skittish virgin bride, a wriggling bundle of firmly locked knees, defensive slaps, and falsetto mewings of mock-terror.

Pashean called his next piece "The Willing Bride on Her Wedding Night." Using the same youth as his stand-in for the bridegroom, Pashean imitated the amorous cooings and heated gasps of a supposedly impassioned woman, and proceeded to climb into his lap and rub the boy's thighs lasciviously. The skit ended decorously enough, with Pashean lying supine, his head nestled in the groom's lap, staring longingly into his eyes.

To my Western eyes, this was exceedingly tame fare, more *Perils of Pauline* than *Sex in the City*, but to the Afghans in the room, Pashean's bodice-ripping farce was heady stuff, and had them gagging and weeping with laughter and embarrassed incredulity.

After a few minutes, Pashean enacted his own death scene. He called it simply "The Death of Samad Pashean." The performance involved Pashean lying prone on the floor in front of us and periodically gasping for an extended period of time before finally falling silent. The death rattle was very authentic.

But then clearly, Pashean was no stranger to death, and afterward, as if to underscore the point, he began bragging about one of the murders he had committed. It seemed that a man had insulted him, and in order to avenge his honor, Pashean had later gone to his home, killed him, and then stolen his shoes. To have made off with his victim's shoes was the height of effrontery—and a very funny thing to do, as well, for everyone laughed uproariously about this.

Next, turning to me, Pashean offered to kill anyone I might want dead in Kabul for the equivalent of two thousand American dollars. When I told him that his price was absurdly high, he guffawed good-naturedly. As I had suspected, Pashean's price was just an initial negotiating position. "We can talk price," he said with a wink.

Like all good jesters, Pashean had some irreverent things to say about the powerful personalities of his country. He singled out Afghanistan's president, Hamid Karzai, for particular disdain. Karzai, he intoned, was like one of the stupid mountain dogs that Afghans keep in their villages, which go off hunting by themselves in the winter only to lose their way home again in the snow. It was a parable that left me flummoxed until my friend interpreted. "Karzai has been with the Americans for so long, he has forgotten what Afghanistan is like."

As Pashean went on, issuing a string of new quips about Karzai—none of them complimentary—I began to discern where he was coming from. Like almost everyone else in the room, Pashean was an ethnic Tajik. Hamid Karzai was an ethnic Pashtun, as were the hated Taliban whom he had replaced. Thanks to the Americans, who had handpicked him, Karzai had become Afghanistan's interim president, but he had been forced to share his government with leaders of the Tajik- and Uzbek-dominated Northern Alliance, whose fighters had swept down from Charikar to seize Kabul after receiving cash, arms, and advice from the CIA. But ever since winning a majority of the votes in the country's first postwar presidential elections— held six months previously—Karzai had purged many of them from their positions and replaced them with his own loyalists.

Pashean accused Karzai of being ungrateful to the men who had fought in the jihad. "The mujahideen are having a hard time now. Karzai is kicking them out from the government. But if people have worked hard for you, you have to give them something in return." He added, grumblingly, that most of the government's U.S.-funded reconstruction projects were taking place in Pashtun areas, rather than Tajik ones, and he asked, "Why are the people who supported the Taliban being rewarded, and not those who fought them?"

Pashean knew how to please a crowd. The men in the room wore aggrieved expressions, and they nodded their heads in agreement with his remarks.

Turning to me again, he brought up the U.S.-sponsored campaign to demobilize and disarm the former mujahideen fighters. Pashean said, "The Afghans are like scorpions, you know, and the Americans are trying to cut off our tails. The Americans are trying to turn the Afghans from scorpions into harmless frogs, but it won't work." Pashean wore a gleeful but challenging expression. "We are turning in only the bad weapons, but keeping the good ones for ourselves, just in case we need them one day in the future." He cackled with laughter, and all the other men in the room did too.

Pashean concluded, "We Afghans have learned how to eat for ourselves, like cows, who, with their cuds, know how to find the good stuff to eat, and how to spit out the bad."

SUGARLAND
~HAITI~

AMY WILENTZ

IN HAITI, PEOPLE ARE OFTEN ON THE BRINK OF STARVATION, SO THEY think about food a lot. Haitians know what they like—it's very specific. They like pork from skinny little Creole pigs, but not from great fat pink American pigs. They like rice grown in Haiti and cooked so that there's some crunchy stuff at the bottom called *gratan* that's burned and sweet. That's the best part, the part "where all the grease, fat, and spices go," a friend of mine says. They like scrawny Haitian chickens that scrounge around and eat what they find; big fat white grain-fed American chickens don't have the right catch-as-catch-can diet for the Haitian palate. Most important, Haitians like food cooked over a charcoal fire. This doesn't mean the food has to be cooked directly on the coals or just above them. Usually, in fact, the food is cooked in an iron pan or a big old pot over the charcoal. But for Haitians, the same thing cooked in the same pan over a gas or electric fire just wouldn't be as good.

Haitians like some strange things, too, but all their tastes are grounded in the idea of the usefulness—and scarcity—of food. Food is not a decoration in Haiti. Haitians, like many malnourished people, are obsessed with foods that are supposed to give you energy, get you through the day. I was once invited to a *tom tom* lunch by a radical priest who is now an adviser to the Haitian government. *Tom tom* is one of many meals said by Haitians to *bay fos*—to give strength. It's an African dish made with very thick, yellowish breadfruit puree. It's my friend's favorite dish. You pick up sticky scoops of the mash with your fingers (already a bizarre thing for a Westerner) and eat it along with a delicious liquid meat stew. You don't even chew the breadfruit. The bits of *tom tom* sink like concrete into your stomach. Haitians like the way those unchewed bits of carbohydrate make even a small meal feel satisfying, but I wouldn't be surprised if an X-ray showed that the *tom tom* I ate at that meal more than a decade ago is still lodged somewhere within.

In August 2010 I went out to the provinces with my *tom tom*–eating friend. We went way up to the northwest reaches of the island, into the profound countryside. We stayed in a church compound—a modest place. I slept on a hard bed and across the room was a big tarantula whose position I checked every few hours in the light of my iPhone (it never moved). I had come to see a gathering of peasants from the surrounding area, and they came in by the hundreds, many of them astride donkeys. For dinner one night, we ate stew prepared by the church ladies. It was delicious, but I kept getting pieces of bone, fat, gristle, and skin. I gave my bowl back to the woman who was serving and asked for some meat, please. The word for meat in Creole is *viann*.

But clearly my understanding of the word was wrong. "You have *viann* there, already," my friend said, looking at the pieces of fat and gristle in my bowl. What I wanted, he told me, was something Haitians call *chèr* or flesh. But the stew had no flesh in it. Flesh is too fancy, my friend told me. Too expensive. The peasants eat gristle, fat, and skin, and sell the flesh in markets down in the towns. Still, the stew was tasty, with three kinds of root vegetables and chicken fat and pasta floating in an intense shallot-flavored broth, and pieces of dense, velvety Haitian avocado on the side.

Two of Haiti's staples are big energy foods: sugar and coffee. Sugar and coffee were grown in colonial times in Haiti and are still grown there today.

The two crops are exemplary of opposite poles in Haitian history and economics. Sugar is a plantation food requiring large tracts of flatlands and intensive labor. Coffee is a mountain crop that can be grown in small individual plots. In colonial days, sugar was grown on the plantations by slaves and coffee in the mountains, by runaways.

Sometimes I think about the first time I was given a piece of sugarcane to chew. This was decades ago, long before the earthquake that struck on January 12, 2010. I remember watching a cane and coconut salesman on the corner of Delmas in downtown Port-au-Prince chopping off a piece of a long, thick brown stick that looked something like bamboo. The traffic was going by, or not going by, and making a huge racket of blasting music and honking horns and talk, talk, talk; shouting, too. I was watching this man cut—and I had eyes only for him. He wore a black button-down shirt that draped over his thin shoulders as if they were a sharp, child-size hanger. He had on long cutoff shorts, and wore black plastic flip-flops on his way gigantic feet. He concentrated on his work and didn't give me a lot of pleasantries, as Haitians normally will do. He didn't want to cut himself with his long knife. He was working away, and it didn't take him long.

Meanwhile, I was watching. He also sold coconuts that he chopped open; I was thinking that maybe that would have been easier to enjoy than this cane. The big green coconuts were sitting in a row, a few piled precariously upon the tops of others. Haitians like to drink coconut water from underripe fruit. Unlike water itself, coconut juice is always clean, and it's sweet and refreshing. This nice man also supplied straws. And you just drank out of the shell. It's easy to drink out of the coconut, and you naturally make the analogy: coconut shell . . . cup. But there was no translating the stick he was cutting into any food or culinary vessel one was used to. You couldn't look at it and say *cup*, or *plate*. As the heat of the traffic jam behind me radiated toward our corner, I was thinking, *This is where the word* cane *comes from*—the hard, brown, upright stalk of the sugarcane plant. (It turns out that the word for sugarcane and for a walking stick and for a rod to punish with all come from the same root: the word *canna,* which is Latin for reed. *Kanasik* is the word for sugarcane in Haitian Creole, from the French *canne à sucre.)*

The sugar man did his work in an instant. He wielded a mean machete, and he did not know—nor did he care—where the word for cane comes from. He handed me a little less than a foot of stick, with the top seven or so inches peeled back to show the dense white flesh. The friend I was with gave the cane man a small amount of change from her purse. He cut a piece of cane for her, too. I looked at mine. It was like something a gardener might know what to do with. *Oh, I'm going to eat this? Yeah, right.* But how, I wanted to know. The friend I was with began to show me. *Comme ça,* she said. And she bent her head toward it. It was a devotional movement.

Is there a way to describe the taste of raw cane? I mean not just *sweet,* but some way to capture the entire experience. Let me try. First of all, wherever you are, if you're eating raw cane, it's hot out, and you're hot and thirsty and this piece of cane doesn't look as if it's going to do much for you. Cane that's ready to be consumed like this is extremely unprepossessing, like a branch of an old tree that some squirrel has knocked down and tried un-successfully to eat, or to kill. It looks mangled, predigested.

So you hold the dry brown stalk in your hand and you dip your head over the exposed inner wood, that's what the white flesh is like, like fresh wood soaked in sugar juice. But until you begin to . . . to . . . to *gnaw* on it, you've got no idea how wet it is, how much juice it holds. You take a bite, and it turns out it's all sugar juice and wood. The thing explodes in your mouth, boom, and you rip the wood away from the stalk with your teeth and chew. You look like a ruminant animal, chewing and chewing, with that stick in your hand so everyone knows what it is you're working over in your mouth. The sugar goes right into your blood, at least it feels that way. The juice sops into your system, and you're rehydrated in an instant.

Meanwhile there's this unpleasantness with the wood. It's like old chew-ing gum—it loses its savor, yet unconsciously, it remains on the scene.

Now you have a mouth full of masticated white stalk, a sort of resistant, woody, tasteless mass that is, at all costs, not to be swallowed. I'd watch other people deal with this: they spat it out on the street, where it rested up against the curb alongside chewed-down mango pits and the split and empty skins of keneps—lychee-nutlike fruits. So I spat mine out—this is not a process that makes one feel delicate and feminine. It's more like being a stevedore or a gangster from the 1930s, spittin' a chaw.

It's hard to eat anything in Haiti without having a political epiphany. Sugar is the king of madeleinelike foods here, a politico-economic treatise in itself. A whole world bursts out of it. Columbus brought the first sugarcane plants to Haiti on his second voyage to the island. After that, the entire colony under the French was involved in sugar cultivation, but the plantation economy could not survive without a slave labor force, and the beginnings of Haiti's slave revolution in 1791 destroyed the economic underpinnings of the trade. By the time the slaves gained independence for Haiti in 1804, many of the French plantations had been burned to the ground and lay in ruins. Small cultivators grew sugar for market and for their own use, but there was no central refinery until the Haitian American Sugar Company was established in 1912. HASCO was one of Haiti's biggest employers, but it has been shuttered in recent decades because Haitian sugar, which is grown by smallholders, has been too expensive to compete with much cheaper Dominican sugar, which is plantation-grown and smuggled into Haiti in large quantities across the border. Even after the earthquake, the cheerful red-and-white HASCO smokestack still stands, smokeless, near the edge of Port-au-Prince. In the 1980s, Haiti exported sugar; now it imports sugar. And who cuts the sugar on the Dominican Republic's sugar plantations? Haitians, the world's best cane cutters, who live in slavelike conditions on huge state-run plantations.

And Haitians cannot stop eating the stuff, as if it were their patriotic duty. I believe that there's more sugar in a cup of Haitian coffee than there is coffee. Their cakes are sweeter than ours. When they make a fruit drink, it's loaded up with sugar. Rum and *klerin* (a supercharged white rum) are favorite drinks, both made with distilled sugarcane. Sometimes the sugar is Haitian—especially the sugar used in *klerin*, which is often homegrown and home-brewed, to say nothing of hallucinogenic. Sugarcane for chewing is also a home-raised crop. It grows by the side of country roads in small patches.

I had a skinny little friend in Haiti who was dating a beautiful and ample woman, a generous, womanly woman. One day I was watching the two of them chat when another friend came up to me, nodded his head at the two, and said in an undertone, *Fòmi pa mouri anba sak sik.* This is one of many succinct Haitian proverbs that come right out of Haitian country life. Figuratively, it means that you can't get enough of a good thing. But literally translated, it means, The ant does not die under a sack of sugar.

There are many other foods redolent of history and politics. Take manioc, a root vegetable that's boiled and mashed and served with meats. It has a sweet, nutty taste. Manioc grows deep in the ground, and when you want to replant a field where it has grown, you have to pull up the whole plant to leave the earth ready for new sowing. This is called *dechoukaj.* When the Duvalier dynasty was overthrown in 1986 and Haitians in crowds went around the country forcing out Jean-Claude Duvalier's henchmen, the slang for the movement was *dechoukaj.* So now when people eat manioc in Haiti, they think about Duvalier.

When you eat conch (*lambi* in Creole), you think of the slaves blowing through the twisty pink shell, which makes a deep honking noise, to herald the beginning of the Haitian revolution and call its leaders together from the plantations. When you eat pumpkin soup, the traditional New Year's Day meal, you think of General Jean-Claude Paul, an alleged narcotrafficker who was killed in 1989 when his holiday soup was poisoned. Rice and beans is such a staple of Haitian cuisine that it is known as *riz national,* and it is as important a piece of the national fabric as the anthem or the constitution. *Griot,* or deep-fried (I mean really deep) pork bits, is so tasty and delicious, so crunchy and amusing, that it has the same name as traditional storytellers, the griots who used to go from town to town, telling complicated stories full of wisdom and jokes from the old country, Africa— where storytellers and songwriters are still called by this name.

You can't *not* think about food when you're in Haiti, about what food is available, where it's available, and who gets to eat it and how often. At the restaurants in Pétionville, the nicer town up the hill from Port-au-Prince, you can get burgers or Bolognese sauce. You can get pâté de foie gras or grilled salmon or take-out spring rolls. You can find flank steak or skirt steak, roast chicken or *poulet Créole.* You can find the flesh that is not in the stew in the countryside.

When I visited in August 2010 I went out in my poncho into one of the refugee camps in the middle of Port-au-Prince's central square during a torrential tropical storm. Like hundreds of others, this camp was slapped up by Haitians made homeless by the earthquake in January 2010. The tarps covering the tin and cardboard shacks were flapping in the wind, and all the adults were inside, taking what shelter they could. Outside, children in skimpy shorts and T-shirts were frolicking. They kicked a soccer ball and made it skip over the water; they rode pieces of cardboard in the streams that were coursing down the camp's narrow alleyways; and they did cart-wheels through puddles that were more like little lakes. They splashed in the base of a decorative fountain that is no longer in service. The grown-ups were grimmer.

I was running down the corridors at sunset, looking for some people I'd met a few days earlier, but I was disoriented in the rain and couldn't find their tent. There was thunder and lightning, very loud, very close. A woman sitting and looking out from a shanty beckoned me in, and I took shelter in her shack. Inside the darkness was slightly relieved by a small flashlight hanging from a piece of earthquake-salvaged rebar. The one-room lean-to was the size of a closet. A narrow, less-than-twin mattress sat on two boxes at the back. This was the house of Jésula Bellevue, who was trying to cook dinner in the rain. (Jésula means "There's Jesus.") Jésula's two little battered aluminum pots sat on top of a small bright red charcoal fire just outside the shack's opening, protected from the rain by a slight extension of the roof that Jésula's boyfriend, Wilner Dorasmé, had somehow fashioned. Wilner was sitting on the bed inside the smoky shack, with a baby on his lap. The baby had a fever. The fire outside cast an orange glow over the interior. Jésula and Wilner's three-year-old son, Walness, laid his head on the side of the mattress and stared at the pot in which his mother was cooking dinner. Behind the pots on the fire, a recent river, created by the storm, was gushing by. Rose-laure, Jésula's eight-year-old daughter, anxiously watched the pot. Roselaure was skinny as a rake in her red skirt and a T-shirt that advertised the country's largest cell-phone company, Digicel. Her hair was done in a dozen tiny pigtails, each ending with a red rubber band. This was to be the family's first meal of the day, and Roselaure was very hungry, she told me. She was bouncing with excitement, and smiled shyly at me every chance she got.

The smell coming from the pot was good, deep and savory. I asked Jésula what she was making. She was making a fish sauce for rice. The rice was already ready, and into the other pot went tomato paste, some mayonnaise, a pat of butter, a stalk of thyme, a can of what Jésula and all Haitians call "salmon" but which, unlike the salmon up the hill, is actually sardines (the can was opened with the family's one knife), and a half cup of rainwater they'd just gathered, plus the rain that was coming down out of the sky into the pot as the sauce cooked. To this Jésula added toward the end one hot red pepper, and an onion ("You want it to stay crunchy," she told me). It was crowded and damp and smoky and dark inside the shack, but with the food coming, it was cozy, too. When dinner was served, the family ate from one plate with one spoon, taking turns.

MY LIFE IN PAGANS

~OSSETIA~

JAMES MEEK

AT A DINNER IN KIEV I HEARD THERE WERE PAGANS IN EUROPEAN Russia. The Soviet Union had just died. After four score years and ten it had gone suddenly, like an old man with heart failure. Without realizing it I was imbibing the nostalgia of the people around me for the safe old broken-down Soviet world, the nostalgia that choked the Russian-speaking lands in the years I lived there. Now I'm nostalgic. I was younger then, but my nostalgia is also nostalgia for nostalgia itself. *Ranshe bylo luchshe* was the refrain in those days: "it used to be better." Though I doubt it did, I miss the regrets of others for the loss of a past I didn't experience, as if fragments of their rosy Soviet memories crept into me and now pretend to be my own.

The host and guests were fastidious intellectuals—academics, I think, or doctors, or engineers, people who drank but abhorred drunkenness, although they might find it amusing in a foreign visitor. There were jackets but no ties. Smart dresses. The women cooked and served. The most far-sighted of them would already have spent every ruble they had on goods and property. The others would lose their savings in the great inflation that was about to hit Kiev like war, like a plague. Hyperinflation and disillusionment would later crush the sort of hospitality I was used to, but then, Westerners were still honored curiosities. We had the aura of little Marco Polos, and nothing was our fault, and we took advantage.

It was a dinner in a Soviet flat, the living room made into a dining room, sofa on one side of the table, chairs on the other, the table covered in cold dishes—a plate of smoked meat; a plate of smoked fish; a salad of diced potato, diced carrot, tinned peas, and mayonnaise; a salad of grated beetroot; a salad of diced vegetables covering an almost raw herring; slippery marinated mushrooms; white bread and butter dotted with orange pearls of salmon roe; pickled cucumbers; pickled wild garlic stalks. There would have been a bottle of vodka, a bottle of sweet red wine, and a bottle of cognac, to be drunk out of dainty cut-glass goblets from the glass-doored cupboard, the *stenka,* that covered one wall. When I was stuffed like a goose the second course would have been brought, pork cutlets or fried chicken with potatoes. Then cake. In Britain and America at this time, the newspapers, one of which I wrote for, were warning of famine in Russia and Ukraine. So were the Russian and Ukrainian papers. The famine was always somewhere the reporter wasn't.

One of the guests began talking about a place in the south, Ossetia, where the people were nominally Christian and actually pagan. They worshipped multiple deities in mountain ceremonies. It was in the Caucasus Mountains. I wanted to go. The mystery of a secret space on the map drew me into the Soviet Union just before it ceased to exist, but Kiev and Ukraine were only partly hidden. I'd had an idea of them before I went. The real lure was the mysteries that didn't advertise themselves until you entered the first mystery, the hidden within the hidden.

I visited North Ossetia, the part of Ossetia that's in Russia, several times after that. It wasn't until my third trip, one and a half years later, that I took part in a pagan rite.

I drove out of Vladikavkaz, capital of North Ossetia, toward the mountains on a bright, hot midsummer's day. Vladikavkaz isn't an Ossetian word. It's Russian, a garrison coinage from the eighteenth century meaning "Rule the

Caucasus," and now it's an industrial city with some pretty czarist quarters, pleasant parks, and swaths of Soviet modernity, a modernity that looks botched and worn-out from the day it is built, yet lasts forever. It seems a regular south Russian or Ukrainian city, that sort of communist-Christian Europeanness, but it isn't. It was the day of the feast of Watsilla, the Ossetian god of the harvest, and the streets were full of portly men in short-sleeved shirts butchering sheep.

The road heads for Kazbek, the dormant volcano that looms over Vladikavkaz. After hundreds of miles of flat Russian steppe the blue rock wall and white peaks of the mountains leap out of the plain with great suddenness. Kazbek is more than fifteen thousand feet high. After an hour of twisting roads we were three thousand feet up, in the steep green alpine meadows of the Karmadon valley. We drove on to Dargavs, location of the holiest shrine to Watsilla, on Mount Tbau. I was to be a guest at the ceremony of the Three Holy Pies, which to the uninitiated would look like a group of men getting drunk and maudlin, making extravagant toasts, and overeating. As for the women, their job was to bake the pies. According to tradition, on this holiday the women had to bake in complete silence. They were supposed to veil their mouths and noses with towels, too, so that even their breath wouldn't hex the pastry; or perhaps it was to stop them spitting in our pies.

Before there could be pies, there had to be a sacrifice. Igor, a vet, took me to a small field around the back of his family's country house. In the pen at the bottom of the field, I saw the holy portion, or rather I saw him seeing us. His eyes reflected a moment beyond fear. Fear implies hope. Here was no hope; here was certainty that the bipeds wanted to kill him. He tried to bolt. Igor seized him by the horns and dragged him up the field to where a table and a basin were set up. The sheep had a brown fleece and a fat tail. Igor threw him on his side on the ground and bound three of his legs with white tape. He hoisted him onto the table with his head hanging over the end, over the basin, and pinned the animal with his right leg, clenching his knee over the sacrifice's stomach. He held the head by the horns, lifted his eyes to heaven, uttered a short prayer, and cut the sheep's throat. Two pints of crimson blood fell into the basin.

Igor let him bleed dry. It took three or four minutes, the sheep twitching all the while. Toward the end he twitched more violently, his legs kicking out.

"If he takes a long time to die, it means the slaughterer has a light hand, and the meat will taste good," said Igor. "If the slaughterer is clumsy, he'll die straight away and the blood won't come out."

Igor untied the legs, cut off the sheep's head, and laid it on the grass. He laid the dead beast on its back and began to gut him, with me holding the carcass to help him. He severed the legs at the knee and placed them with the head. He slit the skin down each leg as far as the main part of the body, then made cuts across the sheep's belly, between the legs, and a lengthwise cut connecting the cuts. He cut delicately around the neck and rump to separate skin and flesh, not getting flesh stuck to the skin and not piercing the fleece. Once the preliminary cuts were made, the flaying was finished by plunging the hand through the sticky filament holding skin to flesh. When the fleece was separate, the sheep's carcass lay on top of it while the butchering was done. Even skinned and headless, the sheep's muscles went on twitching as if it was still alive.

Igor made a careful cut down the belly of the beast, exposing the guts. He tied a knot in the gullet, took out the windpipe, and began to remove the kidney, liver, and heart of the sacrifice.

We did this in the bare mountain light of late morning. No shadow crossed the sun. The Ossetians had a lovely day for their festival, and the mood was joyful. None of them spoke about what had happened in their county-size corner of Russia seven months earlier, in the winter of 1992, after a minority people living within their borders, the Ingush, began agitating for a change of status. Small groups of Ingush men armed with hunting rifles went up against an Ossetian national guard armed, equipped, and backed by Moscow. When the fighting ended, 844 people were dead or missing, most of them Ingush; 64,000 Ingush had been driven from their homes; and thirteen out of fifteen Ingush villages had been destroyed.

There was no fuel at Kiev airport the week of the uprising, and at midnight I bribed my way onto a train to the Caucasus spa town of Kislovodsk, not far from Vladikavkaz. By the time the train had pierced the blizzards in eastern Ukraine and I reached Ossetia, the fighting was over, but the emptied Ingush villages were still burning. I drank tea with happy Ossetians in a row of unscathed one-story Ossetian cottages in a village where, on the other side of the street, the two-story villas of their former Ingush neighbors—fled or dead—were fire-blackened ruins. The Ossetians speak an Indo-European language related to Persian and claim descent from an offshoot of the Scythians, the Alans; Alan is a common first name. I hired a young Alan to help me out. He insisted that he wasn't prejudiced against the Ingush. Some of his best friends were Ingush, he said. It was just that he'd heard they used to be cannibals, and had a genetic predilection for stabbing people in the back. I took him with me to meet some of the Ingush who had been forced to seek refuge among their kin in the eponymous territory of Ingushetia, next door to Ossetia. A Russian federal armored car escorted us across this supposedly internal border. Alan was sure that if the Ingush knew I had an Ossetian with me, he'd be killed. "Don't call me Alan," he said.

The male Ingush refugees pressed in around us, layer on layer, with their stubbly sleepless faces, their gold teeth, and their sheepskin hats. The Ossetians slit open the bellies of pregnant women, they said. They had cut out an Ingush man's heart and made it into an ashtray. They had raped women, raped men, cut off their heads and thrown them to the pigs.

The hotel in Vladikavkaz had an enormous picture window on the stairs looking out over the river Terek toward the bulk of Kazbek. At dusk I saw a Russian helicopter gunship tilt and wheel across the purple face of the mountain. That night I asked the concierge for a glass of tea. She didn't have any, but at the sound of my accented Russian a tall Ossetian guards-man in dark denims with a cut-off Kalashnikov came out from behind a curtain and invited me to his room. He made me tea and we watched a gory Russian film on TV about the seventeenth-century Time of Troubles. On-screen, human heads and limbs flew from the sword blade and women were butchered. The guardsman was courteous and pleasant.

There was a lot of talk from the impotent powers of Boris Yeltsin's Kremlin in the months that followed about enabling the return of the In-gush to their homes, but in the days leading up to the feast of Watsilla, when I talked to Ingush, Ossetians, and the local representatives of federal Russia, they told me that only a handful of Ingush had been able to go back. The Ossetians seemed to feel that the matter was closed. There had been a war—or, as they put it, an Ingush aggression—and they, the Ossetians, had won. Far from casting a dark mood over the holiday celebrations, it gave them more reason to thank their gods. It wasn't about rain anymore. "The Ossetians who gather now don't need a harvest," one of them told me as we were getting ready to drive up to Dargavs. "They're basically city people, so they pray out of respect for their ancestors, and pray for fortune. Health. Success."

At Ossetian feasts, there is a strict order of prayer. In the first prayer the eldest man at table raises his glass of *araka,* maize spirit (it tastes like rough grappa), and appeals to the "great god," the head of the Ossetian pantheon, Khutsau. Each man makes his toast in turn, in descending age order, the youngest last. At my table in Dargavs, at the feast of Watsilla, I was the youngest. The scorched head of the sheep we had killed lay in the middle of the table, with its severed ears behind it, and as the most junior, I had to pick up the ear and bite into it to show that I was humble and listened to my elders. Then I had to make my toast. By this time, the youngest man is so hopelessly drunk that his humility can't be in doubt. I think I managed to string a few words together; I don't remember. The sheep's ear tasted burned, hairy, cartilaginous.

The three sacred pies represent the three essentials of life: sun, water, and earth. They are like flat calzones, some filled with meat, some filled with cheese and beetroot leaves, some filled with potato. The best Ossetian pie I tasted was filled with local white cheese, like a mild feta, with a hot, salty remnant whey trickling between beetroot leaves and pomegranate seeds.

The men were dressed in their holiday best, in well-worn suits. I don't recall what started it, but at a certain point it came out that they were all armed. They began to open their jackets and compare sidearms, boast. One took a big pistol out of his waistband and claimed that it was the only fully automatic pistol in the world, which is to say you could empty the whole clip with one squeeze of the trigger. The oldest man at the table, who was in his seventies, showed us his little gun, the black metal worn away to gray along the edges. Theirs is a martial, patriarchal culture. The commonest religious image in the territory is the god Wastirji, a conflation of a pre-Christian deity and St. George, portrayed as a muscular, bearded man in armor, red cape flowing behind him, on a white horse with a bouffant blond mane, flying out of the sun. Traditionally women wouldn't say his name; they were to refer to him only as the "god of men."

Among the shrines to the Ossetian gods in the valley are shrines of a different kind. It would be wrong to say the Ossetians worship Josef Stalin literally, but they do him honor of a kind that would have been scandalous in other parts of Russia or in Ukraine at that time, in 1993. In Karmadon, there is a silver bust of the Soviet dictator in the public square. Stalin was Georgian, but the Ossetians claim he had Ossetian ancestry. And Stalin was good to the Ossetians.

Beginning at 2:00 A.M. on February 23, 1944, and ending two weeks later, Stalin's secret police rounded up every Ingush man, woman, and child, together with their ethnic kin, the Chechens, loaded them onto twelve thousand cattle wagons, and deported them to Soviet Central Asia. Between the two peoples the total number forced into exile was almost half a million. In the initial roundup 780 were killed; 1,300 died along the way;

and, deprived of their livestock and their usual means of making a living, thrown into an unfamiliar environment in a country whose resources were directed toward war with Germany, as many as a fifth of the deportees—a hundred thousand people—died prematurely in the years that followed.

Among the deportees were Ingush living in what is now part of North Ossetia. Once they'd gone, the Ossetians helped themselves to their land and property. When the Ingush were allowed to return, the two peoples found themselves coexisting in bitterness and mutual resentment only kept in check by the Soviet authorities' rigid enforcement of the appearance of ethnic harmony. For the Ingush, the events of 1992 were a reenactment of the cruelty meted out to them in 1944, by a people who held holy the name of the tyrant who damned them to death on the freezing steppe of Kazakhstan. I talked to one Ingush man who remembered the deportation of '44, when five of his brothers and sisters died of cold, hunger, and disease. He came back to his old village in 1984; now, a few years later, he was in exile again, his home burned, his possessions smashed and stolen.

There was a clarity, at least, to the Ingush sense of injustice. The Ossetians' psychic landscape made less sense. Victory seemed less important to the Ossetians than their ability to convince themselves that they deserved it. They presented the triumph of their armored cars and helicopter gunships over a few farmers with shotguns as a repetition of the Soviet Union's defeat of Nazi Germany. They claimed the Ingush set fire to their own houses before leaving. The Ingush deserved to be deported, they said, because they collaborated with the Nazis. (In fact, there's no evidence that more Ingush were collaborators during World War II, proportionately, than Russians or Ukrainians.) There wasn't much sympathy for Ingush refugees; wasn't North Ossetia looking after tens of thousands of South Ossetian refugees who'd fled another war over the mountains in Georgia?

When I rode up into the mountains with my hosts for the Watsilla holiday, my head was filled with the injustice the Ingush had experienced, the self-serving smugness of the Ossetian authorities, and the vacillation of the representatives of the Russian state of which both sides, in theory, were full-fledged citizens. But I was susceptible to the privilege of the uninvolved outsider, which is not only to accept the hospitality of those for whom conscience suggests hostility, but to accept it without froideur; to embrace it; to enjoy it, and be grateful.

There is a point in the feast when whole Ossetian families, men, women, and children, are together, when the pies and a vast platter of boiled mutton are brought out, steaming fragrantly. A double-handled wooden cup of homemade Ossetian beer, tasting of smoke and honey, is passed around and everyone drinks, the youngest male child first, even if he is a baby. Not long afterward I attended another ceremony at the other end of Europe, in Orkney, off the northern coast of Scotland, where wedding guests took it in turns to drink beer from an almost identical two-handled wooden cup. It was moments like these that made me share the Ossetians' belief that they were a kind of living archaeology, culturally the closest surviving descendants of the horse people who burst out of the steppes of southern Siberia, Russia, and Ukraine to populate Europe in the foredawn of written history; and that the ebb and flow of subsequent invasions stripped them of their horses and squeezed them into one of the narrow valleys of the Caucasus, orphaned, delinquent, always trying to secure their toehold in the fertile flatlands against the competition of their neighbors.

Soviet communism was an ally in that. And the early 1990s must have been terrifying times for the gun-toting old men around that feast table in Dargavs, when a system that had been so kind to them for so long suddenly warped and twisted, when that most delicate of all social relationships, the relationship between being and having, was torn asunder and remade.

Close to where my head was spinning from *araka*, on a ridge near Dargavs hamlet, is the City of the Dead. Squat houses, solidly built of mortared white stone, are topped with beehive roofs made of layers of horizontal tiles, tapering as they rise, each layer separated by stone and cement. Archaeologists are unusually vague about the site, said to have been at the center of a local ancestor cult in the seventeenth and eighteenth centuries.

I'd visited the City of the Dead the first time I went to North Ossetia, less than a year after the collapse of communism. I stood by the doors of the tombs. Ancient corpses in rotting centuries-old clothes lay higgledy-piggledy at my feet. A woman's arm joints poked out of the sleeves of what would have been a fine dress when she was interred. Grave robbers had been at work. The country had gone overnight from the ideal of everything belonging to everyone to the idea that everything had to belong to someone. Everything: oil refineries, hotels, trinkets you could rake from the limbs of the ancient dead.

In Vladikavkaz at that time, the Ossetians were hosting a pan-Caucasian congress designed to show how all the peoples of the region could get along. Young Ossetians, Chechens, and Ingush were dancing together in a hotel restaurant, holding their arms out horizontally like the branches of a tree. There was a Soviet banquet—vodka, sturgeon, platters of cold meat and fish, kebabs—and I drank too much. I suggested that apart from their local languages the Caucausian peoples didn't seem different. Heavy men with sunken eyes I was talking to tilted their cigarettes and looked at me in surprise as they agreed with me, thinking perhaps that I'd saved a few ounces of their conscience for them; usually they had to utter the lie themselves.

On September 20, 2002, a glacier on the northern slope of the Kazbek massif collapsed, sending a crushing flow of mud, ice, and debris two hundred yards wide into the Karmadon valley. Most of the village of lower Karmadon—an area never built on by the ancient Ossetians, who knew better—was destroyed. Among the 125 people killed were a visiting film crew and Russian actor Sergei Bodrov. To this day there is a monument to Stalin in the valley. Fewer than half the Ingush have returned to their homes. On Mount Tbau, the Ossetians still gather each year to honor Watsilla and eat their sacred pies.

THE HOUSE OF BREAD
~BETHLEHEM~

CHARLES M. SENNOTT

IN THE STERILE SILENCE OF CHILDREN'S HOSPITAL IN BOSTON, I AM watching my son Gabriel's vital signs, monitoring every line of his heart rate and waiting for any change in the digital readout of his oxygen intake. By now, my wife, Julie, and I are exhausted and scared. A hospital tray with his uneaten breakfast sits on the nightstand.

Julie stares at the depressing plate of food and begins to read the ingredients with shock, which is quickly followed by contempt. "How do they feed children this crap when they're sick?" she asks, looking at the side of the box of Froot Loops and pointing. "Look at this sugar content!"

She picks up a rubbery piece of white bread that is coated in an unnatural yellow, spongy film of "egg substitute" batter. On the menu, it's called French toast. It looks completely inedible.

"This isn't maple syrup! Look at this, it is just pure high fructose corn syrup. One hundred percent high fructose corn syrup. Really, look at this," she says, putting the little plastic container of syrup in front of me.

But I don't take my gaze from the monitor. She's right, of course. American hospitals provide absolutely horrible food for patients, who, more than any of us, need nutrition and the healing power of good, wholesome meals. This is true even at great hospitals like Children's, which is one of the world's best medical institutions. For Julie, this terrible hospital food devoid of all taste and nutrition is where she is investing her anger. She's railing about the red dyes in the Jell-O and the unbelievable gall and carelessness of offering all the soda and pudding and cookies and Frosted Flakes that kids can get their hands on in the little kitchenette that's open all night. Julie believes in eating well, and our children have for the most part been fed organic and, whenever possible, locally grown food in our home. For sure, I am known to join my boys' chorus of groans over all the tofu and sprouts, though deep down I respect her for the time and energy she invests in helping us all eat healthy food. But at this point I just can't care about it.

My head is somewhere else, and I can't take my eyes off the monitor. I am channeling my rage more in the direction of the doctor at the emergency room at our local hospital who first misdiagnosed our nine-year-old son's stomachache. He sent us home, urging Gabriel to "drink fluids." And he did this even though Gabriel was exhibiting what we now know is every classic symptom of appendicitis. The doctor blew it. And when we got home from the local hospital in the predawn darkness, Gabriel's appendix burst and left him doubled over in excruciating pain. That's when we rushed him here to Children's Hospital Boston. He's in serious condition now with toxins coursing through his intestines and causing intense pain. The battle now is fighting the massive infection, which can be fatal. We are very frightened.

The way Gabriel moaned and winced when he first got here reminded me of the gut shot I once saw a Syrian fedayeen fighter suffer in Kurdistan in March 2003. But this wasn't a war zone and this wasn't a soldier, this was my rail-thin nine-year-old son, with the gentle soul of a poet and boyish dreams of being a boxer. He just didn't deserve a painful blow like this. And all I can keep coming back to is how much I want to strangle the admitting doctor who blew a simple diagnosis for appendicitis. Julie's thinking food, I'm thinking revenge.

In the long, empty silence of a hospital room, Julie and I try to distract ourselves by thinking back to the day Gabriel was born nine years ago. We have four sons and, of course, every one of their births is etched forever in our memory. But Gabriel's birth was the most memorable of all. It was laden with meaning as he was born in the biblical town of Bethlehem in December of the year 2000. We were living in Jerusalem, where I served as the Middle East bureau chief for the Boston Globe.

I was working on a book at the time, retracing the path of Jesus' life in the year 2000. I can feel—and sometimes see—people roll their eyes when they hear we had a child born in Bethlehem in that year of researching the book. The whole reality we were living sometimes felt a bit too contrived. It didn't go unnoticed by my fellow correspondents, who relished teasing us about it. Some jokingly suggested that we might even be suffering from Jerusalem Syndrome, the extraordinary psychosis in which people living in the Holy Land take on biblical characters as part of their persona. There's even a mental ward dedicated to such sufferers in Jerusalem, and in the millennial year the ward was packed with several John the Baptists, a few Marys, and at least one Moses and one Jesus.

The truth about how Gabriel came to be born in Bethlehem is a simple story, but one that got increasingly complicated as time went on. We certainly wouldn't be described as particularly religious, and there was absolutely no conscious level at which we decided to have the birth there for any religious reasons. After all, Julie is from a Jewish family, and I am tribally Catholic, though hardly a practicing one. The reason Julie had chosen the Holy Family Hospital in Bethlehem was that there was simply no Israeli hospital that allowed women to have natural childbirth with a midwife. The Jewish hospital Misgovladak, where our son Riley Joseph had been born nearly two years earlier, had closed. At most Israeli hospitals there was a big focus on high-tech intervention and a high rate of C-sections. At Hadassah in Jerusalem, the nurses took the baby away at night and fed the child formula even if you insisted on nursing. Bethlehem's Holy Family was the only nearby hospital that had midwives and allowed women to nurse through the night. When Julie first made what then seemed like a very rational decision, it was months before the violence of the second Palestinian intifada had really broken out. By the time she had reached her third trimester, the violence was all around us. There were bus

bombings and raging machine-gun battles and the loud thud of tank fire that
could be heard from our home.

As we think back to our son's birth, I can almost smell the tear gas, burning
tires, and cordite that usually accompanied the sounds of fighting at the time. But
mixed among the memory of those bitter smells are mouthwatering aromas, as
comforting to us now as they were delicious then: take-out orders of falafel and
tabbouleh salads of finely chopped bulgur, parsley, and green onions soaked with
lemon and olive oil; the lamb that Julie craved when she was pregnant—typically
seasoned with garlic, rosemary, and thyme, with a hint of the tangy olives on
which the lambs graze in the chalky hills of the West Bank clearly noticeable in
the tender and delicious meat; and, more than anything, soft Palestinian bread,
warm and fresh from the oven.

On November 13, 2000, the Israeli military checkpoint into Bethlehem, the
biblical birthplace of Jesus, was unsettlingly quiet.

Looking back, these were actually the quaint days of foreign reporting
before September 11, 2001, when we still placed "Foreign Press" signs on
our dashboard or taped "TV" on the car doors of our four-wheel-drive vehicles. And we still believed these symbols were as good as white flags or
papers of transport that could get us through almost anything.

On this day, something intangible but ominous hung in the air as we
approached the first checkpoint, and I adjusted the "Foreign Press" sign to
draw more attention to the pretext that I was just a journalist trying to get
through. Julie was eight months pregnant and she had an appointment at
Holy Family Hospital. The decision to have the baby there made sense at
the time, and despite the outbreak of violence we hadn't changed our plans.
That is always what it's like to live in a place that is in conflict. We adapt in
incremental and almost imperceptible ways until the peril surrounds us,
and even then it's hard to see. We just go on living, breathing, and eating
even as the fighting intensifies. It all just seems to be part of life. We had
reasons beyond Julie's preference for natural childbirth and the closure of

Misgovladak. Holy Family Hospital was actually closer to our home in West Jerusalem than the Hadassah Hospital at Mount Scopus. And we liked the obstetrician there, Dr. Nihad Salsa. The nurses were well trained, and no small consideration was the fact that the French nuns who ran the hospital were fantastic cooks. Julie, who was a journalist and documentary producer before we moved to Jerusalem for my job, had volunteered in the orphanage there. She'd come to know the French nuns and Palestinian nurses trained in Ireland and their cooking, which was a perfect blend of local Palestinian recipes with a distinctly European elegance and seasoning.

We were set on having the baby in Bethlehem, but the palpable tension around us was making it seem like a bad idea, particularly on this day. I had a distinctly bad feeling as we rolled to a stop in the long line of trucks and vans packed with Palestinian day laborers. It was quiet and there was no sign of any clashes. But just in case I reached into the backseat of the Isuzu Trooper, grabbed a Kevlar vest, and wrapped it around Julie's pregnant belly, positioning it to best protect her and the baby from possible gunfire. Despite the bad feeling in my gut, we pressed on to our ultrasound appointment with Dr. Salsa.

We rolled up slowly to the checkpoint. The Israeli border guard confidently waved us through, and I felt my nerves settle for a moment. Then at the second checkpoint, near Rachel's Tomb, an Israeli border policeman with a drawn M-16 banged on the hood of the car and waved us back. There were spent rounds littering the road, and the pavement was pocked by gunfire and what appeared to be tank rounds. Rocks carpeted the road from the Palestinian *shabab,* or "boys," who had barraged the post in a demonstration the evening before.

The Israeli border policeman shouted "Y'allah!" and waved us back. It's an Arabic expression that translates as "Go with God," but the Israelis have annexed the phrase and made it sound more like "Move it!" We explained that we had a doctor's appointment and I pointed to my wife's very obvious condition. "Go to hospital in Jerusalem. This is danger here now," the Is-raeli said in broken English with a dismissive wave.

We retreated to the first checkpoint. On our way back we heard a loud explosion to the east near the Palestinian village of Beit Sahour. I later learned that it was a helicopter missile attack on a local leader of the al-Aqsa Martyrs' Brigades, which were largely under the direction of the Abayat tribe, a Muslim clan in this largely Christian town. The Abayats' heavily armed militia had stepped up their involvement in the intifada.

We pulled over to the side of the road and called the doctor to explain that we could not get through. Like all Palestinians, Dr. Salsa had learned over many years to accept the unpredictability of life under occupation, and she and Julie were going over dates to reschedule the visit. But just then the bor-der police started waving the line of traffic through again, so we decided to go forward and try to keep the appointment. We made it. The ultrasound was fine. The baby was due any day. This was our third child, so we were not necessarily new to this drill, but having to navigate a drive to a doctor's ap-pointment through a war zone was a first, and I was increasingly nervous about how we'd get through the checkpoint when Julie went into labor.

I loved the way Julie ate whenever she was pregnant. There was a raven-ousness to it that was wild and joyous and full of life and often involved her buying huge legs of lamb and abandoning any earlier inclinations toward being a vegetarian. On one occasion she had bought an entire lamb from the Palestinian butchers, and the legs and loins and rack of ribs were all wrapped in white butcher paper and stuffed in our freezer.

But as we drove through Bethlehem, Julie said she was craving bread, a simple basket of warm bread. And I knew that a nearby hotel, the Jacir Pal-ace, which was located just before the checkpoint, had delicious Palestinian bread from one of the better local bakeries. So we pulled in. All the excite-ment of getting to the appointment and the great relief knowing that the baby was healthy had made us powerfully hungry. We ordered a meze plate with hummus, baba ganoush, finely chopped tomatoes with thyme, and rolled grape leaves stuffed with rice. We also ordered delicious freshly squeezed orange juice. Julie mostly focused on the bread, working her way through the basket.

The name of this ancient town comes from the Hebrew *beit lehem*, "house of bread." And the town lives up to its name. In the warren of narrow streets that cling to the steep hills of Bethlehem, there are busy bakeries with wood- and coal-fired ovens, or *taboons*, that begin to burn in the predawn darkness every morning. The ovens produce soft, warm layered pita bread and the heartier *taboon* bread, which is baked directly on the hot coals. The *taboons* are round loaves of bread typically about eighteen inches in diameter. I watched with great happiness as Julie pushed the folds of the *taboon* into her mouth and quietly and happily devoured it.

Bread is a universal food, a culinary core that lies at the center of just about all cultures. In our neighborhood in Jerusalem's German Colony, our garden backed up to a kosher bakery just off Emek Refaim Street where we would buy warm challah bread on Friday mornings, standing in line with Israelis doing their shopping before Shabbat. Our children, especially Gabriel, loved challah bread, and in our home outside Boston we traditionally had sweet loaves of challah on Sunday mornings. The wonderful, warm smells of the kosher bakery wafted through our memories of Jerusalem.

In Bethlehem, where tradition holds that Jesus was born, the bread is not just delicious, it also serves as a religious metaphor and a sacrament that lies at the center of the Christian faith. There is, of course, the obvious and laden imagery of the bread of life in Christianity, which harkens back to the Last Supper, when Jesus broke bread and drank wine with his disciples. Bread is also central in the Transubstantiation, which for Catholics means quite literally a mystery of faith in which bread is consecrated and becomes the body of Christ. For the Palestinian Christians who live in Bethlehem this kind of weighty religious idea of bread is about the furthest thing from their minds as they go about their daily routine, which every day involves buying warm, fresh *taboon*. They are not thinking about bread as a sacrament. They're just hungry, and the bread is cheap and delicious. In modern Bethlehem, life is hard under military occupation, but the enduring simplicity of warm, fresh bread is a wonderful and very straightforward part of that daily life.

The Christian Palestinians, who tend to be middle-class, love not only their bread but also finer pastries and cookies that imitate European styles of baguettes and sweet breads. This more bourgeois kind of baking has been brought to the Christian Palestinians through the French, Italian, and German religious orders that have played a role in the Holy Land since at least the Crusades. The cookies in particular are famous. But the core bakery experience for Palestinians is still the warm, pillowlike pita bread, or *taboon*, or the rugged carpets of braided Iraqi bread.

After we had spent about a half hour eating bread in the nineteenth-century grandeur of the old Jacir Palace hotel, the manager came to us and politely asked us if we were finished, as we might want to consider leaving very quickly. He said there was a large demonstration taking shape, and it was about to descend on the checkpoint in front of the hotel. With a grim, weary look, he politely explained that there was almost certain to be gunfire and violence. A waiter wrapped the warm bread in a cloth napkin and guided us to our car, which was waiting out front.

We set out from the hotel entrance, and literally ten yards behind us was the front line of the demonstration. I could see the angry and determined faces of young Palestinian men pushing forward with fists raised in protest. Many were clutching rocks. As we passed the Israeli border guards, they were just loading tear gas canisters into their weapons, and we heard the soft pop of the first volley as it lofted into the crowd, forcing them to disperse into doorways and cover their mouths and noses with kaffiyehs, the signature Palestinian headscarves.

In the next few weeks the intifada raged and reached new heights of violence that stunned us all. I was very worried about having Julie deliver the baby in Bethlehem, and Julie and I agreed that if there was any problem at the checkpoint when she was in labor we would go to a Jerusalem hospital without hesitation.

The monitor suddenly begins beeping, interrupting the quiet of the hospital room and the stirrings of our memory. Gabriel wakes up for a moment and grimaces. His face crumples into a frown. Then he is crying and saying, "It hurts too much. Make it stop!"

At one point, Gabriel keeps repeating, "I can't do this anymore." There is no feeling more powerless than that of a parent who can't console a sick child. Many times I had seen this in the field as a reporter. There were the scenes of Palestinian children wounded in the Israeli military's response to the intifada. And there were the Israeli children screaming in pain in the chaos of the emergency rooms in Jerusalem after a suicide bombing by Hamas. In refugee camps in Kosovo, and in the grimy hospital wards in Iraq, and in rural villages far from any medical care in Afghanistan, I had seen far too many scenes of kids suffering in war. It's always heart-wrenching, but when it is your own child in pain, it is all-consuming. It is the only thing that matters in the world. And I am promising myself never, ever to forget this when I am on a story and see a parent going through this. At Children's Hospital, literally every floor is a level of relativity for anyone with a sick child. Yes, Gabriel is in pain, but we only have to stop in on the cancer ward or visit the trauma unit to realize just how lucky we are to be struggling through a burst appendix. Still, when it's your kid, all relativity is out the window.

The morphine drip is wearing off, and the real pain of what Gabriel is going through is tearing through him again. We ring for the nurse, who hangs a new IV drip for him with more morphine. Slowly he calms down and eventually fades back to sleep. There are more long silences as we watch him sleep, his eyes darting back and forth in some troubled dream sequence he's having. He looks afraid and uneasy in his sleep. I am crying, but then I watch his face grow more peaceful as the morphine envelops and comforts him.

On the afternoon of December 8, 2000, Julie was in labor and we were on our way once again to Bethlehem.

We had worked out an arrangement with a Catholic priest at the Tantur Ecumenical Institute, which is perched on the hilltop just above the check-point. We arranged that we would check in with him when we were on our way. The priest informed us that the checkpoint was quiet and there was no fighting in town. We confirmed this with our dear friend Gerry Holmes, at the time the ABC News bureau chief, who happened to be reporting nearby. So we were on our way, and we sailed through the checkpoint.

As Julie settled in at the hospital, we realized we had made the rookie mis-take of coming a bit too early. But at this point, there was no turning back. I felt strongly that we should not take any chances. So Julie stayed at the hospi-tal and waited for the contractions to intensify. There was a whole different eti-quette for men in the delivery room in the conservative Palestinian culture, and I felt more like an outsider on this birth than on the previous two. Mostly, I smoked cigarettes with an on-duty doctor. We stood in the doorway of the entrance to the hospital and watched a machine-gun battle between the Pales-tinian village of Beit Jala and the Jewish settlement of Gilo just across a valley. Tracer fire lit up the night, and the thud of tank fire sounded like distant thun-der. Julie's room was in the basement of the ancient stone building, and it felt safe and fortressed. We told Julie it was quiet outside, but I have never been able to get anything past Julie, and she looked very suspicious.

"It's gunfire, isn't it?" she asked.

That night I finally checked in to the nearby Bethlehem Star Hotel, with lots of jokes from colleagues covering the story about how there was plenty of room at the inn. When Julie was ready to deliver at last in the early morn-ing of December 9, I was there at her bedside. Gabriel Jerome Sennott was born at 7:35 A.M. He was healthy, weighing in at eight pounds, five ounces.

He had a Palestinian birth certificate issued to him in the hospital, and he would soon have an American passport to back up his American citizenship. The passport listed his place of birth as "Bethlehem, West Bank." But it listed his country of birth as "_____." The space was simply left blank, a legal document that revealed the fact that Bethlehem still did not belong to a recognized state. Palestinian statehood was a matter for what was called "final status" in the peace talks. So Gabriel's birth documents seemed to defy the land's narrow notions of tribe and nationality and even religion. He was listed on his birth certificate as Christian because in Arab culture a child's religion is determined by his father's. But just across the checkpoint he would be defined as Jewish, because under Jewish law his mother would determine his religion. We want our children to love everything about who they are, and we find some mystical meaning in the idea that Gabriel was born in a place that straddles the three faiths of the Holy Land, and in a sacred city that was not yet defined as belonging to any one nation.

After his birth Julie's hunger quickly came raging back, as she was nursing again. Julie's favorite meal at the Holy Family Hospital was *musakhan,* the delicious Palestinian chicken dish served atop *taboon* bread and a layer of caramelized onions and crunchy, sticky rice scraped from the bottom of the pan. There was also a simple, delicious lentil soup, which had the nuns' distinctly French flavorings of lemon and thyme. For dessert there were rice pudding and dried apricots. And, of course, with every meal there was warm *taboon* and pita bread. With breakfast it was served with honey and orange marmalade.

Gabriel wakes up, and he is smiling. It is six days in and he is looking much better as the antibiotics slowly take hold. It's Friday, and when the hospital chaplain, Rabbi Susan Harris, is making the rounds she stops in to see us. She asks about Gabriel and we begin talking about his life and about being born in Bethlehem, and she is very intrigued. She returns later that day with a loaf of challah bread for Gabriel. It's something she does for children on the ward; the loaves are donated by Rosenfeld's Bakery in nearby Newton. She calls the challah bread gifts a "big, cosmic hug." The bread is still warm and perspiring in a plastic bag as she gives it to Gabriel. He smiles and begins eating. This challah is the first thing he has been able to eat in days. He devours much of the loaf, breaking off one piece of the braid at a time and smiling, and we can see that he is finally getting through his ordeal. Rabbi Harris leans over him and offers a blessing, saying, "Be who you are and may you be blessed in all that you are."

On Christmas Eve that year of Gabriel's birth I took his two older brothers, William and Riley Joseph, to Shepherds' Field in Beit Sahour. I was just trying to get them out of the house while their mother wrapped their presents and foraged for a few hours of sleep with the newborn Gabriel. As we drove through the West Bank we saw a shepherd tending his flock. For the boys, all the Christmas Nativity play imagery was always very real and tangible, a part of the landscape in which they lived. We pulled over and walked up into the olive grove to see this shepherd tending to lambs. He was using a wooden staff to knock olives off the branches of a gnarled set of ancient olive trees. The lambs eagerly munched on the olives that landed amid tufts of dry grass in the chalky hills. It was an image straight out of the Bible and an experience I will never forget.

I often found myself questioning these experiences in the context of my faith. I knew it wasn't the religion that pulled me toward them, but I definitely did feel a strong connection to the place, to understanding its reality and trying to get beyond the iconic stained-glass images in the parish church in the Boston archdiocese where I grew up. I wanted to see the living, breathing reality of the land out of which Christianity grew, and the life of the Palestinian Christians who were part of a two-thousand-year continuum of the faith and whose presence was dwindling rapidly in the land where the faith began. I had come to realize that Bethlehem, Jerusalem, the Galilee, and all the datelines of the New Testament were caught in a modern reality that was not unlike the reality two thousand years ago, a place of occupation and violence and a political struggle to control sacred space. I was drawn to the research for my book because of the great layering of history.

Down in Bethlehem that year there was a dark mood. All of the musical and cultural events of "Bethlehem 2000," which was to have been a boon to tourism and the Palestinian economy, were canceled. The traditional Christmas lights strung along the roads leading up to Manger Square were all turned off as a protest by Palestinians against the Israeli-imposed closure of Bethlehem. We stopped at a bakery near Manger Square and bought *taboon* and Christmas cookies. We as a family were celebrating the birth of Gabriel. But the town of Bethlehem was simply not joyous on this Christmas. It was sad and tragic, and we could feel it. As the violence reached a fever pitch in the spring and then into the summer, we knew it was time to leave, so we moved to London, where I had a new assignment for the *Boston Globe*.

A year and a half later, I was back in Bethlehem. The events of September 11, 2001, meant that I was reporting mostly from Afghanistan. The Israeli-Palestinian conflict was raging, and the *Globe* had asked me to return to cover the events, as they were centered on an Israeli military siege of Bethlehem. The Israeli tanks surrounded the Church of Nativity, and Palestinian Muslim militants were holed up inside the basilica with several priests and Christian shopkeepers being held inside the church. It was a thirty-eight-day siege that held the world transfixed. I was covering the story from the edges of Manger Square, and I smelled the bakeries and the warm aroma of *taboon* bread mixed with the conflicting burned smell of cordite from Israeli tank fire. The two smells—warm bread and cordite—mingling together is now my strongest memory of Bethlehem.

On the seventh day, a sleepless, terrible week has finally passed and Gabriel is going home from Children's Hospital. He is doing much better, the antibiotics having finally gained the upper hand against all the toxins in his system. He is slowly realizing that the pain is subsiding. He is beginning to trust that he feels better. When we get Gabriel home, he is treated like royalty by family and friends who've rallied around and helped us get through this rough patch. His brothers are joking with him and making him laugh again. His grandmother, aunts, and uncles are all doting on him. Our yellow Labrador puppy, Bella, sleeps at the foot of his bed. We all love him more than ever and love having him back home, making us laugh as he always does. Julie is cooking for him now. Simple, good food. She brings up bowls of oatmeal with local maple syrup. And she prepares French toast, his favorite meal, only this time it is not rubbery inedible squares like those at the hospital. This time it is made with delicious challah bread from a local bakery and eggs that come from our neighbor's hens. The food is real and it is delicious. It is as simple as eggs and bread and cinnamon, but it is good and warm and Gabriel is devouring it and slowly getting his strength back. He surprises us by asking for more French toast. He is on the mend, and, as it turns out, the thing he wants more than anything else is something so simple and meaningful and a part of his life. He wants bread.

BIOGRAPHIES

JON LEE ANDERSON has written for the *New Yorker* since 1998, reporting from Afghanistan, Iraq, Iran, Lebanon, Somalia, Cuba, Liberia, and many other countries. He has also profiled a number of contemporary political leaders, including Augusto Pinochet, Hugo Chavez, Mahmoud Ahmadinejad, and Hamid Karzai. Among his books are *Che Guevara: A Revolutionary Life, The Fall of Baghdad,* and *The Lion's Grave: Dispatches from Afghanistan.* In 2009, he won an Overseas Press Club Award for a story about life in Rio de Janeiro's gangland.

SCOTT ANDERSON is the author of novels, nonfiction books, and screenplays for films, including *Triage,* which starred Colin Farrell as a war photographer. He writes for magazines that include *Vanity Fair* and the *New York Times* magazine. He is currently working on a book about T. E. Lawrence.

JASON BURKE is the South Asia correspondent of the *Guardian.* He has been reporting from the subcontinent since the mid-1990s, excepting a few years working in the Middle East. His 2003 book, *al-Qaeda: The True Story of Radical Islam,* sold more than seventy thousand copies in Britain and has been translated into twelve languages. A second book, *The Road to Kandahar,* followed. A third book, a contemporary history and investigation of the wars, militancy, and campaigns against terrorism that have marked the first decade of the twenty-first century, will be published in 2011.

RAJIV CHANDRASEKARAN, a senior correspondent and associate editor of the *Washington Post,* is the author of *Imperial Life in the Emerald City,* a best-selling account of the troubled American effort to reconstruct Iraq. The book, which provides a firsthand view of life inside Baghdad's Green Zone, won the Overseas Press Club book award, the Ron Ridenhour Prize, and Britain's Samuel Johnson Prize. It was named one of the 10 Best Books of 2007 by the *New York Times* and was a finalist for the National Book Award. He has served as the *Post's* national editor and as bureau chief in Baghdad, Cairo, and Southeast Asia.

BARBARA DEMICK is the Beijing bureau chief of the *Los Angeles Times* and a former Seoul correspondent. Her book *Nothing to Envy: Ordinary Lives in North Korea* won the BBC Samuel Johnson Prize for best nonfiction in 2010 and was a finalist for the National Book Award.

JANINE DI GIOVANNI is an award-winning writer who has reported from war zones for twenty years. The author of four books, she is widely anthologized, and two documentaries have been made about her life and work. Her next book, *Ghosts by Daylight,* will be published by Knopf in 2011.

FARNAZ FASSIHI is the Beirut bureau chief for the *Wall Street Journal* and author of *Waiting for an Ordinary Day: The Unravelling of Life in Iraq.* Fassihi has been reporting in the Middle East for more than a decade and covered the wars in Afghanistan and Iraq. She served as Baghdad bureau chief for the *Journal* for three years. She won six national journalism awards for her coverage of the 2009 Iranian election and uprising, including the Robert Kennedy Award for best international reporting and the Hal Boyle Award from the Overseas Press Club.

JOSHUA HAMMER, *Newsweek's* Jerusalem bureau chief between 2001 and 2004, is now a freelance foreign correspondent based in Berlin. He is the author of three books, including *A Season in Bethlehem: Unholy War in a Sacred Place.*

TIM HETHERINGTON was a writer, photographer, and filmmaker whose documentary film *Restrepo* won the Grand Jury Prize at the 2010 Sundance Film Festival and was nominated for an Oscar. He was killed while working in Libya in 2011.

ISABEL HILTON is a London-based writer and broadcaster whose work has appeared in the *Sunday Times,* the *Guardian,* the *Independent,* the *New Yorker, Granta,* the *New York Times,* the *Los Angeles Times, El Pais,* the *Financial Times,* the *Economist,* and many other publications. Her particular interests include China, South Asia, and Latin America. She is the author of *The Search for the Panchen Lama* and appears regularly on the BBC.

LEE HOCKSTADER spent thirteen years as a foreign correspondent for the *Washington Post* in Latin America, the former Soviet Union, Europe, and the Mideast. Now a member of the *Post's* editorial board, he lives in Washington with his wife and two children.

SAM KILEY is a writer, a broadcaster, and the author of *Desperate Glory: At War in Helmand with Britain's 16 Air Assault Brigade.* He has worked for the *Times* of London, the *Sunday Times,* the *London Evening Standard,* and Britain's Channel Four. In 1996 he won Britain's Granada Foreign Correspondent of the Year award for his coverage of the fall of Mobutu's Zaire. He is the security editor for Sky News.

CHRISTINA LAMB is the Washington bureau chief of the *Sunday Times* of London and author of several books including the best-sellers *The Africa House* and *The Sewing Circles of Herat.* She has won Britain's Foreign Correspondent of the Year award five times. Her latest book, *The Wrong War,* will be published in 2011.

MATT McALLESTER grew up in Scotland and lives in New York. As a correspondent for *Newsday* he covered numerous conflicts. He is a visiting professor of journalism at the City University of New York, a freelance magazine writer, and the author of three books, including a memoir of his mother, *Bittersweet: Lessons from My Mother's Kitchen.*

JAMES MEEK was for many years a foreign correspondent for the *Guardian* and is the author of four novels, including *The People's Act of Love,* which has been translated into twenty languages. He was named Britain's Foreign Correspondent of the Year in 2004.

MATT REES is an award-winning crime novelist and foreign correspondent who lives in Jerusalem. Rees covered the Middle East for a decade and a half for *Time* magazine and *Newsweek.* His series of Palestinian mysteries won the Crime Writers Association New Blood Dagger and has been published in twenty-three countries. His latest book is *Mozart's Last Aria,* a historical novel about the death of the great composer.

CHARLES M. SENNOTT is the executive editor and cofounder of GlobalPost, a Web-based international news organization. He is the author of three books, including *The Body and the Blood: The Middle East's Vanishing Christians and the Possibility for Peace.* A longtime foreign correspondent and Middle East bureau chief for the *Boston Globe,* Sennott has reported from more than thirty-five countries, including Afghanistan, Iraq, Kosovo, and Israel-Palestine.

WENDELL STEAVENSON is the author of two acclaimed books, *Stories I Stole,* about Georgia, and *The Weight of a Mustard Seed,* about an Iraqi general and the morally compromising times of Saddam Hussein. *The Weight of a Mustard Seed* was named a notable book of 2009 by the *New York Times.* She has written about the Caucasus and the Middle East for many publications, including *Time* magazine, *Slate,* the *Financial Times* magazine, the *New Yorker,* and *Granta.*

AMY WILENTZ is the author of *The Rainy Season: Haiti since Duvalier,* and of *Martyrs' Crossing,* a novel. She is a professor in the literary journalism program at the University of California, Irvine, and a former Jerusalem correspondent for the *New Yorker.* She writes about Haiti for the *New Yorker* and other publications.

ACKNOWLEDGMENTS

The writers in this collection all showed immense generosity, patience, energy, and forbearance, not to mention their great talents, and I am as grateful as anyone could be. Thank you. This is your book.

Flip Brophy, Felicity Rubinstein, Judy Heiblum, Sheila Levine, Darra Goldstein, Kate Marshall, and Emily Park made the book happen. They were all hugely kind and supportive. My friend Jen Banbury helped form the original idea.

My wife, Pernilla, was my greatest ally, as always. And in the midst of my collecting these tales of war and food our son, Harry, arrived in the world, fulfilling a million dreams and creating a million more.

The loss of contributor Tim Hetherington has left many who loved him somewhat lost for words. We are lucky to have his wonderful words in this collection.

CALIFORNIA STUDIES IN FOOD AND CULTURE

DARRA GOLDSTEIN, EDITOR

DESIGNER
SANDY DROOKER
TEXT
9.5/14.75 SCALA
DISPLAY
AKZIDENZ GROTESK
COMPOSITOR
WESTCHESTER BOOK GROUP
PRINTER+BINDER
THOMSON-SHORE, INC.